SUSHI MADE EASY

Made Easy

by Nobuko Tsuda
foreword by Donald Richie

New York · WEATHERHILL · Tokyo

Photos by Katsuo Meikyo

The assistance of the Nakano Vinegar Co., Ltd., producers of Mitsukan Vinegar, and the Tokyo Mutual Trading Co., Inc., Tokyo, is gratefully acknowledged.

First edition, 1982

Fourteenth printing, 2002

Published by Weatherhill, Inc. of New York and Tokyo. © 1982 by Nobuko Tsuda; all rights reserved. Printed in the U.S.A.

Library of Congress Cataloging in Publication Data: Tsuda, Nobuko. / Sushi made easy. / includes indexes. / 1. Cookery (Fish) 2. Sushi. I. Title / TX747.T74 641.5952   AACR2 / ISBN 0-8348-0173-6

Contents

Foreword

Japan, an archipelago surrounded by seas, is a great fish-eating nation. Almost none of the foods coming from the ocean is considered inedible, and some of these—squid, octopus, and the many varieties of ocean fish—are eaten in enormous quantities. Seaweed, various shellfish, sea urchin, shrimp and prawn—all are eaten, but the national favorites are those meaty fish found in the Pacific: tuna, mackerel, bonito, sea bream.

These are prepared in an enormous variety of ways. They are boiled and broiled, steamed and grilled, pickled and fried, dried, and served fresh. Among all these, however, the most popular method of presentation is the last—fresh, that is, raw.

Fresh seafood is served in two major manners. Sliced and appropriately decorated, served in a bowl or on a dish, it is called sashimi and is often the first course of a typical Japanese meal. An even more popular method, however, is when it covers fingerfuls of rice and is a meal in itself. This is sushi.

One of Japan's most representative foods, sushi is now known around the world. Most large cities in America and Europe have sushi shops and the dish has been described in *The New York Times*.

Here is Craig Claiborne's definition: "An assortment of small morsels of freshest raw fish and seafood pressed into cold rice lightly seasoned with vinegar." This is a perfectly servicable description so far as it goes, but it does not go far enough. Sushi, a delight to the eye as well as a revelation to the tongue, is also an engrossing culinary happening that those who have tasted will not soon forget.

It was not always such, and, as is the case with so many beloved foods, its beginnings are somewhat unappetizing. Originally, it appears that what we now know as sushi was merely preserved fish. Rice was packed round the uncut fillets and was then thrown away before the aging flesh was eaten. There is, however, a more elegant accounting of the origin of sushi from the same period. The *Nihon*

Shoki, an official history of Japan compiled at the beginning of the eighth century, says that the twelfth-generation emperor, Keiko, was served raw clams dressed with vinegar and liked them so much that he made the inventor, Mutsukari no Mikoto, his head chef. Thus, it is said, did early Japan establish its predilection for fresh seafood.

Nonetheless, fish preservation continued, and it is from this combination of seafood and rice that the present-day sushi evolved. Over the centuries layers of fish and layers of rice in a jar with a stone on top turned into a food itself. The resultant fermentation gives the sharp sweet taste that vinegared rice now approximates, and the whole is still called *nare-zushi** and still eaten, rice and all, in the country.

This dish became in turn what is still known as Osaka-style sushi and remains very popular in that city. Fresh seafood is put into a shallow mold, rice is added, and the whole is pressed. The result is a kind of large pie that is then cut into bite-sized pieces.

The kind of sushi with which the world is now familiar, the more popular Edo-style of finger-formed *nigiri-zushi* described by Craig Claiborne, is a rather late development, having been originated in Tokyo (then Edo) in the early nineteenth century. There is no fermenting, no pressing into molds, no waiting. Whatever its fast-food origins—it was said to have originated to facilitate Kabuki customers, famished but not wanting to miss the beginning of the third act—it has now become the supreme type of sushi.

(It should perhaps be noted that here, as elsewhere so often in Japan, the name gives little clue to either origin or history. Sushi is written with two characters, but the characters themselves vary, though their pronunciation remains the same. *Su,* meaning "vinegar" is sometimes seen but this is apparently a very late variant. More often the *su* is *ju* (in its Chinese reading), which can mean "long life" or something equally felicitous. The *shi* is most often the Chinese reading of the Japanese character *tsuka,* which can mean "to control" or "to arrange." However, Japanese being Japanese, "arranging for a long life" would not be the proper translation of sushi. In the event, though *kanji* character readings of the name are sometimes seen, most often the sound is simply rendered in the syllabic *kana* form, which has no more meaning attached than to the separate letters of our alphabet. Thus is the difficult task of "reading" characters often solved. It may thus be said that sushi has no translation.)

*Sushi is pronounced zushi when suffixed to other words.

Having come into its own, nigiri-zushi proliferated into a number of forms, all now available at the sushi shop and most capable of being made at home as well—and all in addition to the finger-formed bite-sized standard.

In one variation, a square of seaweed is swiftly coated with rice, something is put in the middle, *wasabi* (Japanese horseradish) is added, and the whole is rolled into a long cylinder that is then cut into pieces or eaten as is. If pickled dried gourd is used inside, the result is called *nori maki;* if cucumber, *kappa maki;* if strips of fresh tuna, *tekka maki;* if omelet and seafood mixed, *datè maki,* and so on.

Or, the seaweed is rolled on the bias to make an ice-cream-cone-shaped sushi called *temaki-zushi.* Or, vinegared rice is packed into a bag of fried tofu, and the result is *inari-zushi.* Or, the rice is wrapped in dwarf bamboo leaves and called *sasa maki-zushi.* Or, a favorite to make at home, seafood is shredded over a bowlful of vinegared rice, and the dish is called *chirashi-zushi.* And there are many other variations as well.

Sushi proper, that is, nigiri-zushi, comes in the widest of choices. In order of their probable popularity there are: tuna (*maguro*), the marbled underside of the tuna (*toro*), the half-marbled side section of the tuna (*chu toro*), sea urchin (*uni*), boiled or live shrimp (*ebi*), sea bream (*tai*), squid (*ika*), ark shell (*akagai*), young yellowtail (*hamachi*), adult yellowtail (*buri*), octopus (*tako*), salmon roe (*ikura*), conger eel (*anago*), abalone (*awabi*), and many other seasonal fishes and shellfish, ending up with the only nonseafood item in the lot—*tamago yaki,* a bit of thick, sweet omelet on rice. There are, in addition, regional specialties, some of which use fresh-water fish. There is the slightly bitter *funa-zushi* from Shiga Prefecture, which uses the carplike *funa,* the fish said originally preserved back in the old days when the rice was thrown away. Toyama has *masu-zushi* made with trout, and Kyoto in the sum-mertime has *ayu-zushi,* fresh fillets of the small, salmonlike *ayu* on rice.

All of these varieties and many more are popular. In fact, sushi has been called the most popular food in Japan. In Tokyo alone there are between ten and fifteen thousand sushi shops—in all of Japan there may be one hundred thousand such establishments. In addition, sushi is often served in the home as a special treat. If we conserva-tively estimate the number of families in Japan as twenty-five million and if each serves sushi once a week, we then have a tremendous amount of it being consumed.

There is thus no specialized clientele for sushi, as there is in the

West, where, though popular, it is by no means yet a national food. Everyone likes it, and the amount eaten is determined only by the amount of money one has to spend on it, because, for a national passion, it is surprisingly expensive.

Despite (or because of) its expense, however, a mystique has grown up around sushi. Though the masses may gorge on just any old fresh fish with rice, the sushi aficionado (a character somewhat like the connoisseur of French cuisine or of wines) picks and chooses, both subject to and at the same time contributing to the many stipulations that create the sushi mystique.

He knows, for example, that seafood raw should be eaten only at its freshest. Thus he himself has it only for the midday meal or earlier and much deplores those who sup on sushi or, worse, have it as a late-night snack. By this time, as the connoisseur well knows, the seafood is no longer fresh enough to please the discerning palate.

The discerning palate also knows the very best sushi shop—the one no one else knows about. He knows what fish are in season and consequently freshest. He also knows the master and always asks his advice. How is the tuna today? Had he better stick with maguro, or might he venture the chu toro, or is today one of those fine days when he may go all the way with toro itself? Master and connoisseur discuss the possibilities and then, with gravity and responsibility, make the choice.

This sushi *tsu* (a word denoting a person of extreme knowledgeability) will also, of course, know the proper language, since the sushi mystique insists upon a separate vocabulary. In addition to knowing all the proper names of the various varieties, he will also know that one does not call soy sauce *shoyu* but rather *murasaki;* that ginger is in the sushi shop not called *shoga* but *gari;* that wasabi is *sabi* (or even *namida*—tears—because this native horseradish is so piquant); that tea is not *ocha* but *agari;* and that when he asks for the bill he does not call for the usual *kanjo* or the ordinary *dempyo* but the much more elegant *oaiso.*

For every tsu, of course, there are hundreds of ordinary sushi-lovers who consume this favored delicacy anyplace, at any hour of the day or night, if they can afford it. Sushi, being comparatively expensive, however, is not an everyday treat.

The expense varies. At the sushi shop where you order each variety as you want it the cost is greatest. If, however, you order a predetermined selection, a *moriawase,* then the price declines, if only because it does not contain much, or any, expensive salmon roe or marbled underside of tuna. Rather, it contains what is seasonal and hence less expensive. Sushi is a seasonal food, and its cost depends upon what is available (and what is not). Winter fish (herring) are cheap enough in February but very expensive in August, for example. The moriawase are relatively less expensive because they are largely made of those seafoods presently in season.

Most sushi shops, even the best, make a large part of their profit from these moriawase, because it is these that constitute the takeout orders and such must comprise at least half of the shop's business. If you want to have people over to the house and want to serve a gracious snack, you call up the corner sushi shop and order several moriawase. In a very short time the boy on his bike appears with the order nicely packed in lacquer trays or boxes (to be returned later) along with murasaki, gari, and even chopsticks (though the tsu always uses his fingers—but then a tsu would not be eating a moriawase).

Or the lady of the house may decide to make her own. This is the least expensive of all sushi. She buys the seafood at the local store, where the fishmonger cuts it properly for her. Back home she prepares the vinegared rice, assembles the other ingredients, and does it all herself.

Such homemade sushi tastes very good indeed, but the hostess always makes apologies for it. The sushi mystique demands that it be made by an expert, and, indeed, sushi-making is an intricate art. More often she will settle for chirashi-zushi, all the ingredients sprinkled over a large bowl of vinegared rice, a single-dish meal to which everyone helps himself. This is delicious and filling and takes little skill to make, and the mystique is not applicable.

A visit to the sushi shop itself will indicate the degree of skill necessary and perhaps the reason why the sushi *itamae* are given the same kind of reverential regard that the West accords, say, French chefs.

The sense of occasion that distinguishes sushi-eating begins as soon as one walks into the shop. Behind a long counter of immaculate white cypress is a glass-cased, ice-cooled array of seafood, all unmistakably fresh and some alive. This colorful decor, both pristine and crisp, offers the eye an overture of delights to come. Behind it stands the sushi itamae and his assistants, all in cleanest white, ready to perform one's bidding.

After an apprentice has brought a cup of piping hot tea, a dish for the murasaki, a moist *oshibori* hand towel, and pinches of gari with which to refresh the mouth between bites, one is ready to order.

Some prefer an hors d'oeuvre of freshly cut sashimi accompanied by beer and/or hot or iced sakè. Others want to begin directly with sushi. The itamae, upon hearing the order, gets busy with fingers and knives, and the performance begins.

Deft and skillful, each stroke swift and precise, he cuts and slices, scoops a double fingerful of rice, adds a bit of sabi and swiftly forms the oblong ball, seafood now firmly in place. A piece of sushi thus properly done has, it is said, all the grains of rice facing in the same direction. Acquiring this technique, say the masters, requires many years.

Two such "fingers" of sushi constitute an order. To eat them one may use the chopsticks provided, but the more knowledgeable do not. They pick up the piece with the fingers, turn it over, dip the seafood side lightly into the soy sauce, and then convey it to the mouth. Marveling at the succulent freshness, one then regards the itamae at work on the next order, in due time calling out one's own.

Becoming a full-fledged sushi itamae and owning eventually one's own shop is a long and exacting process. One might think that slicing up fish and putting the pieces on rice fingers was a simple enough procedure, but not at all.

The apprentice often begins at the sushi shop as soon as he finishes secondary school, that is, when he is seventeen or so. He washes up and carries the takeout orders for a number of years, and then he is allowed to help with the daily making of rice.

This is itself a skill. Good sushi rice must be glossy and have a certain chewiness to it. It is thus cooked with less water than ordinary rice and the water is hot to begin with. After the proper amount of seasoned vinegar has been added, the cooked rice is put into a large, shallow wooden tub made of Japanese cypress and is spread with wooden paddles, since anything made of metal might make the vinegar react. It is then tossed and again spread, cooling all the while. The techniques involved are not simple, and the apprentice ought spend a number of years learning them.

In the meantime he has been observing the master at work. Cutting seafood for sushi is more an art than a craft. One's technique at the carving table must be impeccable, to be sure, but each piece of tuna is different from any other, and its grain and consistency must be observed before it is cut. It is here that the art comes in. Watching the itamae at work, cutting and slicing swiftly and unerringly with his number of knives, one might think only a certain dexterity is required. Not in the slightest. Between each lightning stroke there is calculation, deliberation, choice.

All of this the apprentice, now an assistant, must observe. Later, he will himself practice. Finally, he will receive his license from the itamae and be ready to appear on his own as a full-fledged *sushi-ya*. In due course he may expect either to continue with the master or to open his own shop.

This method of learning is one shared with other Japanese arts. Apprentices to the woodcarver, to the Kabuki actor, to the metal-worker, and to the stonecutter undergo similar training. Watch and imitate—this is how a Japanese art is learned. One understands eventually not only the techniques but also the all-important attitude of the master toward his discipline. It is the attitude that makes the master—and also contributes considerably toward the mystique of sushi.

At any rate, it is said that the tsu, ferreting out new sushi shops, looks first at the apprentices. If they are alert and busy, watchful and obliging, if they put out more hot tea without being asked, at the same time keeping a learning eye on the shop master, then the chances are that the attitude of the place is proper and that good sushi may be the outcome.

How then can the non-tsu, knowing nothing of any of this, pick the proper place to enjoy this not inexpensive delicacy? He can begin by making it a rule never to have sushi in a place that does not serve only it. Sushi in ordinary restaurants, cafeterias, and the like is always bad—the only bad sushi one runs the risk of eating in Japan. Therefore, always repair to the sushi shop. But which, among the thousands available?

The Japanese, of course, would never approach the problem in this fashion. They would instead go to a sophisticated friend and ask his opinion. Then, after some consideration, the friend would name a shop that had his trust and probably his patronage. Better, he might take the inquiring friend there himself and introduce him. Indeed, to the best shops of all, as to the best bars, an introduction is necessary.

If one has no knowledgeable friends, then trial and error is the only solution. In general an old shop is better than a new one, and a small shop is better than a large one. There is also one other con-sideration—price. Any sushi shop in Japan serves very good sushi, but really extraordinary sushi costs. One way of determining the potential price is to observe the sushi shop sign or window. Inex-pensive places, those listing the prices, are well worth the visit, and those serving the finest and the most expensive sushi list no prices at all.

The oaiso, the bill, is another important element entering into the sushi mystique. Though perhaps beginning as a fast food, it has now become—at the best places—the most expensive cuisine in Japan. A meal at a first-class sushi shop costs twice as much as a full steak dinner, and everyone knows how expensive beef is in Japan.

The reason is, of course, that the best shops serve the best fish, and the days are now long gone when tuna frolicked in Tokyo Bay. Nowadays a fresh tuna at Tokyo's Tsukiji fish market can cost thousands of dollars, and enough of the marbled underside of a tuna to make four servings costs well over twenty-five dollars. And these prices are wholesale—without overhead and profit added.

So, be prepared for something special when the itamae totes up the bill. (This, as befitting his near sacerdotal status, he does with expected panache: he has memorized just what every one of his twenty-some customers has had and with calculator swiftness writes the amount on a small slip of paper that he discreetly hands over.) A hundred dollars a person is quite ordinary. In a really fine shop the bill can come to much more. One can also, however, eat fairly well for twenty-five dollars, but do not expect superb marbled tuna.

The first-class shops serve only freshly caught seafood. Other shops serve seafood flown into Japan, usually frozen: sea urchins from Los Angeles, prawns from Mexico, squid from Africa, herring and tuna from the Atlantic. Some tastes survive the journey. Others do not.

This means that the master and his assistants must be expert shoppers as well. The itamae goes to the fish market himself, early in the morning, and makes the earliest and best choices. He takes only the finest portions of the day's catch and rejects far more than he purchases. He will know exactly which fishmonger, among the hundreds in the entire market, to go to for which seafood. He will probably not take part in the fish auctions held daily, because he will already have made his purchase privately earlier.

Finally, loaded down, he and his assistants will return to the shop and begin the day's work, preparing for the early morning tsu who wants his breakfast straight from the sea.

There is in Japan at present a general concern about the price of sushi and the (un)availability of materials. One representative recently said: "With raw material costing so much, the traditional sushi industry cannot survive." This representative, to be sure, was connected with the traditional sushi shop's greatest rival, a vast fast-food chain devoted to sushi. This outfit, Japan's largest and far outdistancing such petty foreign rivals as McDonald's, Mister

Donut, and Colonel Sanders, has almost two thousand sushi outlets in Japan, and last year it showed a profit of almost sixty-three billion yen.

Its "secret," says the representative, is to use the best possible Japanese ingredients (they do not define "possible") coupled with American merchandizing and marketing techniques. Buying in massive bulk, they are able to charge less per item, and mechanization cuts down on expensive labor. And, as for the apprentice system and the making of nigiri-zushi, well, "anyone can learn to make sushi in ten days." So much for the tsu.

So much as well for the ambience, the skill, the dedication, the technique, and the art of sushi-making at its best. Still, the majority of sushi shops in Japan are as yet privately owned, and they seem nearly always to be filled. At least a part of the population remains willing to pay high prices in return for the complete sushi experience: taste, sight, decor, performance, bill, and all. So long as such customers survive, so will the art of sushi.

As for the taste and savor of sushi, it is always good and (since you cannot eat mystiques) easy enough to enjoy even at home. First, you go to the fish market....

Donald Richie

SUSHI MADE EASY

Ingredients and Basic Preparations

The repertoire of sushi chefs is expanding at an amazing rate, and chefs at home, experimenting with new combinations of ingredients, are creating many new sushi dishes. Given this situation, it is easy to see that the compilation of a complete list of sushi ingredients is an impossible task. Therefore, the ingredients included here are only those featured in the recipes that follow. You may find foods that are new to you; you may also be surprised to come across familiar ones.

Once you've decided which dish you'd like to prepare, consult this list when you are selecting the required ingredients and utensils. In cases where substitution is possible, specific recommendations have been included. Most of the ingredients that appear are probably at your local fish market or sitting on the shelves of a well-stocked supermarket. A trip to an Oriental provisions store will turn up any that are not. For illustrations of many ingredients and utensils, consult pages 15, 16, 33, and 34.

Vegetables, Dried Foods, and Liquids

Bamboo Shoots (*Takenoko*)
The tender shoots of the bamboo plant are harvested only between March and May. Cut into pieces, fresh shoots, with their unique crunchiness and aroma, are a gourmet's delight. When fresh shoots are not available you can use dried, bottled, or canned varieties. In a few simple steps the preserved varieties can be made to taste almost as good as fresh shoots. Preserved shoots often have a white substance clinging to the pieces, or suspended in the canning water. This is not harmful but it does detract from the shoots' appearance and taste. To get rid of this substance, wash the shoots in fresh water and boil them for 2–3 minutes. Bamboo shoots should be cooked and seasoned before eating.

Seasoned Bamboo Shoots

150 grams bamboo shoots, cut into bite-size pieces
1 scant cup stock no. 2 (page 6)
1/2 teaspoon salt
2 teaspoons sugar
1 teaspoon mirin
2 teaspoons soy sauce

Mix the liquid ingredients and the salt and sugar in a saucepan. Add the cut bamboo shoots and cook over low heat until the liquid is reduced by half. Remove the pan from the heat and allow to cool before using.

Bean Curd (*Tofu*)

Bean curd, or *tofu*, has become the center of much attention among Western cooking enthusiasts. Besides containing supremely nutritious vegetable protein, the delicate taste and custardlike texture of this soybean product has found its way into many new and interesting Western dishes as well as some familiar ones, for example, hamburger patties and cheesecake. In Japan, it is one of the staples of the traditional diet. Eaten as is with a variety of flavorings or cooked in any number of ways it is a delicious accompaniment to any Japanese meal.

The ivory cakes of fresh bean curd themselves are not used when making sushi, but two types of cooked bean curd are. A thin slice of bean curd that has been deep-fried (*abura age*), seasoned on the sweet side, is used to form a small pouch that is stuffed with sushi rice and other ingredients to make Fox Sushi (page 104). It is available at most Japanese food shops, either fresh or in cans. *Kori-dofu* (or *koya-dofu*) is the freeze-dried cousin of the familiar bean curd cake. The bean curd used to make freeze-dried bean curd is denser than the bean curd that is eaten fresh. It is also richer in protein. Freeze-dried bean curd is readily identifiable by its sponge-like appearance. When buying it, select those that are light yellow in color, finely grained and lustrous, and light in weight. Most freeze-dried bean curd has to be reconstituted before eating, but there is also an "instant" freeze-dried bean curd on the market that can be cooked as it comes out of the package. Sometimes this instant variety comes mixed with seasonings or a soup base to which you add boiling water to ready it for use. Like several other sushi ingredients, freeze-dried bean curd must be cooked and seasoned before eating.

Seasoned Freeze-dried Bean Curd

4 pieces freeze-dried bean curd
1 2/3 cups stock no. 2 (page 6)
2 tablespoons sugar
2 tablespoons soy sauce
1 tablespoon mirin
1/2 teaspoon salt

Place bean curd in bowl and cover with boiling water. Use a saucepan lid that fits inside the bowl to keep the bean curd submerged. Once the pieces are well soaked and soft, press them between your hands to squeeze out the water, making sure not to tear or crumble them. Repeat this operation until the water that comes out of the bean curd is clear. Combine stock, sugar, soy sauce, mirin, and salt in a saucepan and add the reconstituted bean curd. Boil over low or moderate heat for about 10 minutes. (Here, too, set a small lid inside the saucepan to keep the bean curd submerged.) Cool to room temperature. Cut to desired size.

Bonito Shavings (*Katsuo-bushi*)

The shaved flakes of dried bonito, called *katsuo-bushi,* are very aromatic and tasty. They can be eaten as is, sprinkled over a hot bowl of rice, for example, but most importantly they are used, along with *kombu,* to make the basic Japanese stocks called *dashi.* To prepare a bonito fillet for shaving, it is first boiled in water to rid it of all fat and oil. Then it is smoked and dried repeatedly until it becomes rock hard. A seeding with mold completes the process. Flakes can be obtained from the hardened fillet in two ways: either shave the fillet on a special plane fitted into a box or simply buy preshaved flakes, called *hana-gatsuo* or *kezuri-bushi.* Shavings of bonito should not be confused with those of mackerel pike or horse mackerel. The flavors of these do not compare in any way with that of bonito shavings. Whether you shave the fillet yourself or buy packaged flakes, the shavings cannot be kept for too long or they will lose their flavor and aroma. Therefore, shave the fillet just before using and keep the preshaved flakes in an airtight package in the refrigerator. If packaged flakes are unavailable, a stock concentrate, which comes in powdered or liquid form, can be substituted. It is used just like instant bouillon preparation. The methods and ingredients for making stock differ according to what it is to be used for. Stock that is the base for a clear soup must necessarily be more carefully seasoned than one that is used for cooking vegetables.

In either case, high quality kombu and bonito shavings are essential for making delicious stocks.

Stock No. 1, for clear soup (*ichiban dashi*)

4 cups water
10-cm-square piece of dried kombu
10–15 grams bonito shavings

Bring the water to a boil in a saucepan. Wipe the kombu clean with a damp cloth. Make a few slashes in the leaf with the tip of a knife and drop in the boiling water. (If you have time to spare, allow the kombu to soak in the water overnight before placing it on the stove.) Just before the water reaches the second boil remove the kombu and set it aside. (It will be used again in the next recipe.) Reduce the heat and stir the shavings into the hot water. Remove the saucepan from the heat. Strain the stock through a sieve lined with a cotton cloth. Set the shavings aside. (They will be used again in the next recipe.)

Stock No. 2, for cooking vegetables and miso soup (*niban dashi*)

Combine the kombu and bonito shavings leftover from the preparation of stock no. 1 in a saucepan with 3 1/3 cups of water. Place the pan over high heat. Just before the water reaches full boil remove the kombu. Lower the heat. Simmer over low heat until about 20% of the water has evaporated. Strain through a sieve lined with a cotton cloth.

Burdock (*Gobo*)

A member of the aster family, this long, slender root vegetable is harvested year-round. But burdock pulled out of the ground in early spring is considered the tastiest. The fibers and slight bitterness of burdock are said to be highly effective in preventing geriatric disorders. To bring out its flavor, burdock is simmered in a seasoned stock.

Seasoned Burdock

200 grams unpeeled burdock
1 scant cup stock no. 2 (page 6)
2 teaspoons sugar
2 teaspoons mirin
1 tablespoon soy sauce

Scrape off the skin of the burdock with the backside of a knife. If the burdock is very slender, cut the root into thin slices. Otherwise, cut it lengthwise into two or four parts before slicing. Boil the burdock slices in water until they become tender. Mix the remaining ingredients in a separate saucepan. Add the tenderized burdock slices and simmer until the liquid is reduced by half. Cool.

Deep-fried Bean Curd Slices, see Bean Curd

Devil's-Tongue Jelly (Konnyaku)
Konnyaku is the grayish brown or pale gray cake of gelatinous paste made from the processed tuberous corms of the devil's tongue plant. It is made up almost wholly of water and is very low in calories. Besides being an ideal food for dieters, it also contains calcium and is alkaline. It is available fresh, canned, or in instant form at most Japanese provisions stores.

Dried Sardines (Niboshi)
Sun-dried sardines, called niboshi, are used for preparing a stock similar to but more strongly flavored than stock made with bonito shavings (page 6). These small, silvery fish are rich in protein and calcium. The best are distinguished by straight whole bodies that glisten and feature a slight touch of green on the spine.

Dried Sardine Stock

4 cups water
15–20 grams dried sardines

Snap off the heads and belly parts of all sardines. Split each fish in two lengthwise. Rinse lightly in water and place in a saucepan containing cold water. Place pan over heat and bring to a boil. Boil for about 6–7 minutes, constantly skimming the surface for impurities that rise to the surface. Strain. Adding a 10-cm-square piece of kombu to the water and then removing it just before the water boils will greatly enhance the flavor of this stock.

Eggs (Tamago)
The slightly sweet flavor and bright yellow color of an omelet serves to balance the taste and appearance of a sushi meal. Just as there are many varieties of sushi so there are many ways to prepare eggs to complement this rice dish. But, in general, only three styles are used, all of them omelets: a thin omelet, a rolled omelet, and a

thick omelet made with ground fish meat. These omelets are usually cooked in the special square omelet pan described on page 46. But a standard round frying pan about 25–26 cm in diameter (and not too heavy) can be used in its stead. The recipe that follows gives instructions for making a thin omelet with a conventional frying pan.

Thin Omelet .

6–8 omelets

4 eggs
1 1/2 teaspoons salt
1 teaspoon sugar

Beat the eggs and add the sugar and salt. Mix well. Heat the frying pan until it starts to smoke. Oil the surface of the pan. Remove any excess oil. Pour a generous amount of the egg mixture into the pan (1). Tilt the pan over the heat, thus coating the entire surface with the egg mixture (2). Pour the excess egg mixture back into the mixing bowl (3). Cook over moderately high heat, tilting the pan from side to side so only the outer edges of the pan come into contact with the heat (4). Once the outer edges of the omelet are cooked, the center will also be done—without a scorch! Remove the pan from the heat and turn the omelet over with your hands (5). Cook the reverse side just long enough to dry and set the omelet's surface (6). Remove the omelet from the pan and allow it to cool to room temperature on a flat surface. Repeat this procedure until all the egg mixture has been used. Once cool, the omelets can be cut to any desired shape.

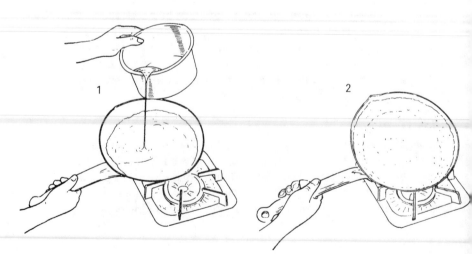

1

2

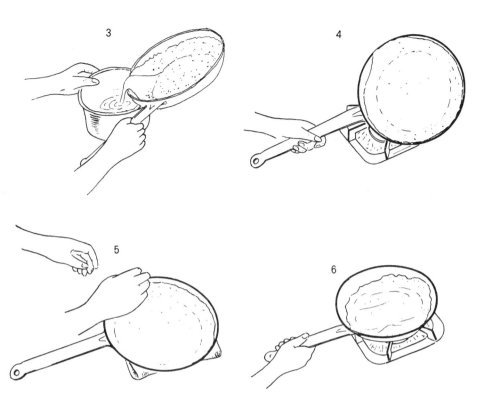

Rolled Omelet

This type of omelet is used in many varieties of sushi. It can also be served by itself; a thin slice, secured with a narrow strip of nori to a finger of sushi rice, and a thick slice of rolled omelet are colorful additions to a plate of finger sushi.

5 eggs
2–3 tablespoons stock no. 1 (page 6)
1 teaspoon sugar
1 teaspoon mirin
1/2 teaspoon salt

Mix all the ingredients in a mixing bowl. (Some cooks strain the eggs through a cotton cloth to obtain a finer texture.) Make sure the salt and sugar dissolve. Heat a square Japanese omelet pan until it starts to smoke. Evenly oil the pan with an oil-soaked cloth (1). Remove any excess oil. Pour in about one quarter of the egg mixture (2). Once it has set, fold it toward you in two steps (3). Lightly oil the exposed pan surface (4). With chopsticks or a small spatula, move the folded omelet to the far end of the pan and lightly oil the exposed pan surface. Pour another quarter of the egg mixture in the pan (5), making sure some seeps underneath the first roll. Once it has set, roll the first rolled section toward you over the cooked egg (6–7). Oil the pan, move the roll to the far end of the pan and repeat the procedure until all the egg mixture has been used. Remove the rolled omelet from the pan and place it on a bamboo rolling mat. Press with the rolling mat to give the omelet a rectangular shape.

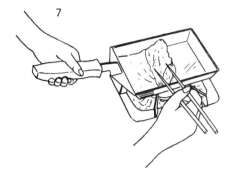

Thick Omelet with Ground Fish Meat

This omelet is heartier that a rolled omelet but is used to top finger sushi in the same way.

5 eggs
70 grams white fish meat, or a pounded fish-meat preparation
called *hanpen,* if available
1/2 teaspoon salt
2 tablespoons sugar

In a mixing bowl, beat the eggs well. Add the salt and sugar. Grind the fish meat (or hanpen) in a grinding bowl and add to the egg mixture. Heat and oil a square Japanese omelet pan over moderate heat. Pour in the egg-and-fish mixture and cover. Reduce the heat and cook for about 10 minutes, or until the omelet has set. Remove the lid and turn the omelet over with a spatula. Cook the reverse side for a few seconds to set the omelet.

Freeze-dried Bean Curd, see Bean Curd

Ginger Root (*Shoga*)
The root of the ginger plant is familiar to most Western cooks. It plays an important role in Japanese cooking, lending a touch of sharpness and aroma to many dishes. This is particularly true of sushi. When eating sushi pickled ginger slices called *sudori shoga* (*gari*, in the jargon of sushi fans) are always served. Taken between bites, it freshens the palate so you can fully savor the unique taste of each type of sushi. When making sushi at home a good supply of pickled ginger slices is essential.

Matchstick-size strips of ginger root that have been soaked in water for five minutes, called *hari shoga*, are used as a garnish in many foods. Pink-dyed ginger strips, called *beni shoga*, are also a familiar garnish. To make beni shoga: peel and slice ginger root. Blanch the slices in salted boiling water. Soak in the juice of umeboshi until they turn pink. Slice into strips and use as desired. Yet another pickled garnish is made from ginger stalks. This is called *hajikami shoga* or *fude shoga*. Recipes for pickled ginger slices and stalks follow.

Pickled Ginger Slices

50 grams fresh ginger root, peeled
Marinade
3 tablespoons rice vinegar
2 tablespoons stock no. 2 (page 6)
1 tablespoon sugar
1/2 teaspoon salt

In a bowl, combine the vinegar and stock. Add the sugar and stir until dissolved. Set aside. Peel and slice the ginger root as thin as paper. Soak in cold water for about 5 minutes. Blanch the slices in salted boiling water for 3–5 seconds. While still hot, add the slices to the vinegar and stock marinade. Marinate for at least 30 minutes. Drain the slices and serve. Pickled ginger slices can be made in quantity and refrigerated for future use.

Pickled Ginger Stalks

ginger stalks, 7–8 cm in length
marinade for pickled ginger slices, enough to cover the stalks

Prepare the marinade as for pickled ginger. Blanch the stalks in salted boiling water. While still hot, add the stalks to the marinade. Once the stalks have turned a pale pink they are ready to eat. These can be made in quantity and refrigerated for future use

Kampyo

The ribbonlike dried strips of the calabash or bottle gourd are called *kampyo* in Japanese. If they are of good quality, the strips are well-dried, white in color, of uniform thickness, and have a slightly sweet fragrance. When selecting shavings, avoid those that are slightly brown, a sign of age, or unnaturally white, an indication that they have been bleached. Such shavings do not approach the taste of fresh, unbleached shavings. Before using these for cooking they must be tenderized and seasoned.

Seasoned Kampyo

20 grams kampyo
2 1/2 cups stock no. 2 (page 6)
4 tablespoons sugar
2 tablespoons mirin
2–3 tablespoons soy sauce
1 teaspoon salt

Rinse the kampyo strips thoroughly. Sprinkle them with salt and knead gently. Soak in tepid water for about 10 minutes. Boil the kampyo in the soaking water until soft and tender. Drain. Place the tenderized kampyo in a medium-size saucepan. Add the stock and bring to a boil. Add the sugar and mirin and simmer for 10–15 minutes. Add the salt and soy sauce and simmer for another 5 minutes. (As the time required for the kampyo to absorb the flavors varies, the procedure is staggered.) Drain and cool to room temperature.

Kombu

Kombu, or kelp, thrives only in the coldest sea water. The dark brown leaves are harvested during the summer. After a thorough drying in the hot summer sun they are cut, folded, and sealed in airtight packages. Kombu is rich in glutamic acid, calcium, iodine, and iron. This versatile leaf is also shaved into paperlike sheets which are called *oboro kombu.* Sheets of the shaved white heart of the leaf are called *shiraita kombu.* The dark, dried leaves of this seaweed are among the basic ingredients of the stocks that are used in cooking many Japanese foods. As is true with most basic ingredients, when purchasing kelp it's best to pay a little more for a higher quality product.

Leaves (*Ha*)

Cutout leaves are used to separate different kinds of sushi when they are arranged together. They keep the different tastes from mixing, prevent the sushi from discoloring, and add an accent of color to the arrangement. The large leaves of the bamboo plant have been used widely since olden days for wrapping food and as a decoration. This led to their use in sushi. Aspidistra leaves are also used to decorate arrangements of sushi at sushi shops. When these are not available almost any leaf will do as long as it is clean and free of pesticides (maple leaves are particularly elegant). Nowadays artificial cutouts of plastic are available, but as these are not nearly as attractive as real leaves their use is not recommended. It's better to do a little searching in your own area to find leaves to accent your sushi creations.

There is a special knife for making leaf cutouts but a small, sharp knife will produce equally good results. To cut a shape from a large leaf, wet the underside of the leaf so that it will stick to the cutting surface. Hold the leaf down with one hand and cut the shape with the other, holding the knife near the tip of the blade as if grasping a pencil. For symmetrical shapes, fold the leaf in half before cutting.

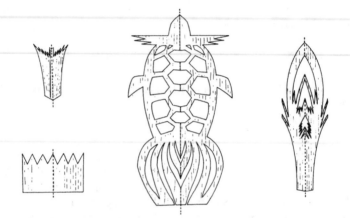

Lotus Root (*Renkon*)

The crunchy root of the lotus plant can be cooked in a variety of ways: simmered with vegetables, dressed with vinegar or sesame seeds, or deep-fried as tempura. It is also used in rolled sushi and scattered sushi. It is rich in vitamin C. If you are lucky enough to be there when tubers are harvested in the early fall, those nearest the plant are the most delicious. Lotus root is obtainable year-round and can be stored for a considerable length of time, but once cut, the root must be used within a few days or else it will turn brown and unsightly and lose its distinctive flavor.

To prepare lotus root, first pare it. Cut or slice the white meat to the required size and shape and then soak it in water acidulated with 1–2 tablespoons of vinegar to prevent it from discoloring and to rid it of any harshness in flavor. When boiling the lotus root, add a

Packaged dried foods and liquids: 1. rice vinegar, 2. dark-colored soy sauce, 3. light-colored soy sauce, 4. mirin, 5. sakè, 6. rice, 7. dried sardines, 8. fried bean curd, 9. umeboshi, 10. sea urchin paste, 11. sea urchin, 12. green tea, 13–14. toasted nori, 15. kombu, 16. dried bonito, 17. bonito shavings, 18. freeze-dried bean curd, with soup base, 19. shiraita kombu, 20. oboro kombu, 21. kampyo, 22. shiitake, 23. wasabi paste, 24. pink-dyed pickled ginger strips, 25. instant vinegar dressing, 26. white sesame seeds, 27. black sesame seeds.

Vegetables: 1. takuan, 2. coltsfoot, 3. green beans, 4. snow peas, 5. lotus root, 6. cultivated mountain yam, 7. burdock, 8. shiso, 9. wasabi, 10. carrot, 11. spinach, 12. cucumber, 13. bamboo shoots.

small amount of vinegar to the water. Care should be taken when boiling the root, because it will lose its whiteness and crunchiness if boiled for too long.

Mirin

Mirin is a sweet wine made from various kinds of glutinous rice. It is one of the basic ingredients of the vinegar dressing for sushi rice, adding aroma, a touch of sweetness, and a pearllike luster to the finished product. There are two types of mirin, *hon mirin* and *shin mirin*. Their flavors are slightly different, but either can be used for making sushi rice. When mirin is not available a pale dry sherry, in a lesser amount than what is called for, can be substituted. Sugar can also be used in its stead but only in an emergency—mirin does more than simply sweeten sushi rice, it deepens the flavor, something that sugar cannot do.

Mountain Yam (*Yamaimo*)

The long, hairy, mountain yam is both found in the wild and cultivated. The latter variety is commonly called *nagaimo*. Eating this yam is said to be good for digestion and to help lower high blood pressure. The gluey, yet crisp quality of the mountain yam makes it a very delicious combination with cod roe and bonito shavings in Hand-rolled Sushi (page 98).

To prepare this vegetable for eating, peel it rather thickly and soak it in vinegared water for 20–30 minutes to eliminate any bitterness. Generally speaking, the thicker portion of a yam is the tastiest.

Natto

The fermented soybean product called *natto* has a very distinctive aroma and is quite glutinous. It often makes an appearance in the traditional Japanese breakfast. Like most soybean products, it is highly nutritious.

Nori

Sheets of dried laver, called *nori*, are used for rolling up vinegared rice and a number of other ingredients to make many varieties of sushi. To make sheets of nori, seaweed is gathered from the sea, washed, and then chopped into small pieces. After being washed in fresh water to remove any salt, the pieces of seaweed are then poured into a large, square frame and dried. The sheets that result are cut into manageable sizes and packaged. A nutritious food, nori is rich in vitamins A, B_1, B_2, B_6, B_{12}, C, and D, as well as iodine, and has been shown highly effective in curbing the formation of cholesterol deposits in blood vessels.

When selecting nori for sushi, look for sheets that are absolutely dry, highly aromatic, smooth to the touch, shiny and dark, and of even thickness. Sheets with holes or that are brown in color will not do for rolling sushi. Oftentimes, nori comes in a bundle of ten sheets (each sheet measuring 20.5 × 17.5 cm) folded in two, the "front" on the outside, and sealed in cellophane.

Lightly toasting nori over an open flame will greatly enhance its flavor and aroma and make it crisp. To toast, place two sheets, "back" sides out, together, and pass them over an open flame. Repeat this procedure with the "front" sides out. Once toasted, nori absorbs moisture quickly, so don't wait too long to use it after toasting.

Oboro Kombu, see Kombu

Rice (*Kome*)

The taste and texture of cooked rice is central to the sushi experience. Thus the selection of the proper type and quality of this all-important ingredient must be made with great care. Because rice is cultivated over a wide area there are innumerable brands and types to select from. But this should not deter you. Simply stated, the best rice to buy is white, short-grain, Japanese rice that comes in a package marked "for sushi." A well-stocked Oriental provisions store will be your source for this. But, if none is available, the second choice is simply white, short-grain or long-grain rice. Instant rice will not do. Newly harvested rice should be avoided because it tends to be sticky when cooked. Older rice is considered the best. If new rice is all that is available, simply reduce the amount of water when cooking. For more specific instructions on how to cook rice, see page 48.

If you are in a quandary about which rice to choose, watch for grains that seem somewhat transparent and that are generally equal in size. Avoid grains that are marked with white streaks or cracks.

Sesame Seeds (*Goma*)

Sesame seeds add flavor and aroma to several sushi dishes. White sesame seeds are the most common, but black and yellow varieties also find their way into some dishes. Sesame seeds are rich in calcium, vitamins B_1 and E, and polyunsaturated fatty linolenic acids.

While it's fine to use sesame seeds as they are, roasting them enhances their characteristic flavor and aroma. To roast, simply heat a small frying pan, toss in the seeds, and, stirring constantly, warm them until three or four seeds have jumped. By that time they should have turned a golden brown. Remove the seeds from the pan immediately.

Shiitake

In its natural state, the *shiitake* mushroom grows on the trunks of pasania, chestnut, and various species of oak trees. In recent years, this relatively large species of mushroom has come to be artificially cultivated. It contains ergosterol and vitamin B_2, and it has been discovered that a substance found in this mushroom checks the increase of cholesterol in blood vessels. Although fresh shiitake are delicious, dried ones are used when preparing sushi. This is because the mushroom's taste and aroma increases with drying. When selecting dried shiitake, make sure they are thoroughly dried, feature a hood that is brown and slightly glossy, are short-stemmed, and have a rich aroma. The thicker the hood of the mushroom, the better the taste and aroma. The price of dried shiitake varies according to how well the mushrooms are formed, not according to their size and taste. If small pieces are called for in a recipe, buy the cheaper brand with less perfect shapes. To augment the taste of shiitake, they should be cooked and seasoned prior to use.

Seasoned Shiitake

10 pieces, about 10 grams each, dried shiitake
4–5 tablespoons sugar
4–5 tablespoons soy sauce
4 1/2 teaspoons mirin

Rinse the mushrooms with water and soak until they have returned to their natural shape and become soft to the touch. (The time required for them to reach this state varies, but 30 minutes is usually sufficient.) Cut off the stems. Place the reconstituted mushroom hoods in a small saucepan and add enough of the soaking water to cover. Bring the water to a boil. Reduce the heat and simmer for 2–3 minutes. Add the sugar and soy sauce. Simmer until the liquid has evaporated, stirring from time to time to keep the mushrooms from sticking to the pan. Add the mirin and rock the saucepan so that the boiled-down liquid adheres to the mushrooms. Cool to room temperature and cut to desired size.

Shiraita Kombu, see Kombu

Shiso

Shiso, a member of the mint family, is known in the West as perilla or beefsteak plant. There are two species of shiso that are eaten in Japan, one with green leaves and stems and another with purplish red leaves and stems. Shiso is rich in vitamins A and C and also contains substantial amounts of calcium, iron, and phosphorus. Green-leaf shiso has a unique aroma and taste and is used in many varieties of sushi, in dressed, saladlike dishes, and in tempura. Red-leaf shiso is used for coloring umeboshi, ginger, and various other Japanese pickles. The shiso plant, with its beautiful serrated leaves, reaches maturity in the summer. The delicately colored flowering seed pods are used as a garnish on a plate of sashimi.

Soy Sauce (*Shoyu*)

Soy sauce is the familiar rich, brown sauce made from a fermented mixture of brine, wheat malt, and soybeans which is called *shoyu* in Japanese. While the taste of soy sauce may differ from brand to brand, generally speaking there are two basic types: the dark-colored *koi kuchi shoyu* and the light-colored *usu kuchi shoyu*. The latter is less fragrant and contains more salt. Not so popular in Japan is a third type called *tamari*. It is much thicker and has a stronger soybean flavor than either of the two more common types of soy sauce. Dark-colored soy sauce serves for almost all home cooking and is used to season many dishes. It is also the type of soy sauce served with sushi.

The soy sauce that is available outside Japan is most often of the dark-colored type. It stays fresh longer, thus retaining its flavor, if it is kept in a cool, dark place.

Takuan

Takuan is a pale yellow or pale brown pickle made from a large, white *daikon* radish that has been dried and pickled in rice bran and salt. It is named after the famous Zen priest Takuan (1573–1645), who was the first to make it. Takuan can be eaten as is, or it can be desalted and fried in oil. It is available at Oriental provisions stores in either canned form or in large barrels filled with rice bran and salt. Avoid purchasing takuan that is artificially colored bright yellow.

Trefoil (*Mitsuba*)

Three species of trefoil, a perennial member of the parsley family, are eaten in Japan: *kiri-mitsuba, aka-mitsuba,* and *ne-mitsuba*. Often referred to simply as *mistuba*, trefoil is a highly aromatic plant whose stems and leaves are used to accent the flavors of many foods and as a garnish.

As soon as possible after purchasing trefoil, place the cut ends of the stems in a glass of cold water. This will keep the leaves from wilting and retain the trefoil's distinctive aroma. Add trefoil to a soup only after you have turned off the heat; when using it as a soup garnish, add trefoil to the soup bowl just before serving.

Umeboshi

Umeboshi is the dark red, salted pickle made from a species of plum. The piquant taste of umeboshi goes well with sushi rice. To make umeboshi, green plums, still quite hard, are pickled in brine; red shiso leaves are added for flavor and color. This mixture is covered with a weighted lid and left to sit for a month or so. The half-pickled plums are then dried in the sun and again packed away in the brine mixture for yet another month. What results is one of the staples of the traditional Japanese diet. It can be found in bottled form in nearly every Oriental provisions store. *Bainiku*, a preparation of pitted umeboshi that has been flavored with mirin is also available in bottled form.

Bottles of umeboshi and bainiku, once they are opened, should be kept in the refrigerator. There they will keep almost indefinitely.

Vinegar (*Su*)

Rice vinegar is, without doubt, the single most important flavoring in sushi. It perfectly complements the taste and texture of cooked rice and the tang of wasabi. The fragrances of wine vinegar and apple vinegar are too overpowering for sushi; they would obliterate the delicate flavors of the dish. What is more, rice vinegar has many nutritional benefits, not the least of which is that it aids digestion. It also acts as a disinfectant. Before you handle sushi rice, it's a good idea to drench your hands in a solution of vinegar and water. The rice will be much easier to handle and your hands will be all the cleaner.

The mild taste of rice vinegar is fast becoming a favorite of many Western cooking enthusiasts. It is available in nearly all Oriental provisions stores.

Wasabi

Wasabi has the power to efface the smell of fish. It is an absolute must for making finger sushi (page 63) and mixed with soy sauce makes a delicious sauce for sashimi.

A perennial plant of the coleseed family indigenous to Japan, wasabi grows along the banks of pure, cold streams. It grows only 3 cm a year, taking several years to reach maturity. In Japan, it is cultivated in mountain terraces through which mountain water is allowed to run. It is claimed that the sharp taste of wasabi stimulates the stomach, helps digestion, and neutralizes any poison.

Fresh wasabi that appears pasty and green in color is the best. When grating wasabi, wash it clean, pare away the brownish skin and remove the eyes, and grate from the part nearest the stalk. Use wasabi immediately after grating it because once grated it begins to lose its bite. For the same reason, grate only enough at one time to meet your immediate needs.

Fresh wasabi is hard to obtain in the West, but there are sub-stitutes—a powdered version and one that comes in a tube. The first is simply mixed with water into a thick paste, covered, and allowed to sit for a few minutes to reach its tangy peak of flavor. Wasabi in a tube is used simply as it comes out. Once opened the tube variety should be kept in the refrigerator.

Beware: Western horseradish is neither aromatic enough nor delicate enough in taste to even be considered as a substitute.

Fish and Shellfish

Fish and shellfish destined for being eaten as sushi must first and foremost be fresh. This is because in most cases they will be eaten raw. Knowing how to assess the freshness of a whole fish, pieces of fish meat, shellfish, and so on will improve your chances of finding the freshest, and therefore most delicious, fish at the fish market or the best preserved frozen fish at the supermarket.

Freshness is of particular concern when considering whole fish, that is, those fish shipped with their internal organs intact. When examining such fish make sure that the scales are intact and glossy; the flesh, resilient; the eyes, black and clear, not bloody; the belly, firm; the gills, bright red. And, there should be no fishy smell! Bloody eyes and blackish gills are sure signs that the fish must be cooked before being eaten.

When buying cuts of fish meat, make sure that the meat is firm and has a sheen, and that the blood at the cut or sliced sections is vivid red. As washing fish meat in water leaches its flavor and makes the flesh crumbly, it's best to buy a whole fish and dress it at home. How to do that will be described shortly.

Once you have purchased a whole fish, it should be dressed as soon as possible. Once dressed it must be kept cool. If it is to be used within a short period of time, place it in your refrigerator after covering it with a damp cloth. If the dressed fish is to stay refrigerated for more than half a day, seal it in plastic wrap. If left uncovered, dressed fish will dry out in the refrigerator.

The taste of frozen fish depends on how well or how poorly it has been thawed out. The very best way to thaw frozen fish is to place it overnight in your refrigerator and allow it to thaw out gradually. But, if you are in a hurry, thaw out the frozen fish in salted water: if it is a freshwater fish, place it in a solution of 4 cups of water and 1 1/2 teaspoons of salt; if it is a saltwater fish, 4 cups of water and 1 tablespoon of salt. This will check most flavor loss. Do not, however, thaw out the frozen fish completely. Once it can be cut with a knife it is sufficiently thawed out to use.

Filleting a fish for sushi can be done in one of two ways: the three-part method *(sanmai oroshi)* or the five-part method *(gomai oroshi)*. Following the three-part method one ends up with two fillets and a skeleton, and following the five-part method, four fillets and a skeleton. The three-part method is used for fish shaped like sea bream, mackerel, or gizzard shad. The five-part method is for flatfish such as flounder. The two methods are the same except for the final cutting away of the fillets, therefore only the three-part method will be detailed with illustrations.

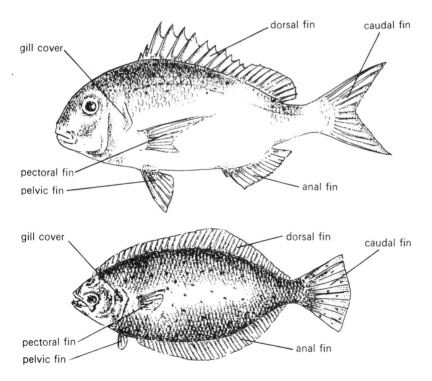

23

Three-part Method for Filleting Fish

Dampen both sides of the fish with a wet cloth. This will make scaling easier (1). Hold down the head of the fish firmly with the left hand and scrape off the scales with a knife or scaler held in the right hand, moving from tail to head (2). Repeat the process on the other side. When handling the fish, always hold it by the head or the tail to keep the flesh firm. Place the head of the fish to the left with the belly facing you. Lift up the pectoral fin and thrust the knife underneath it and make an incision in the direction of the pelvic fin (3). Remove the head. Remove the entrails, by hand if necessary (4). Next, wash the fish clean in salted water, especially the cavity made by the removal of the entrails. Wipe the fish dry with a cloth. Place the fish diagonally on a cutting board with the belly facing right and the tail towards you. Cut from the pelvic fin toward the tail. Turn the fish over. Insert the knife through the back, so that the blade grazes the rib cage, and cut from right to left, all the way to the tail (5). Turn the fish 180°. With the point of the knife, cut through the bones that form the top of the rib cage (6). Separate the fillet from the body. Turn the fish over, bone side down, and cut the meat free from the backbone, slicing from the tail to the head (7). Turn the fish 180°. Cut the meat at the base of the tail free from the backbone. Separate the fillet from the body. Cut off the bones of the rib cage that are still attached to the fillet (8). Place the fillet on a cutting board with the tail end to the left and the skin side down. Make an incision at the base of the tail end, grip the skin of the tail end with your left hand, insert the knife between the skin and the meat, and with a sawing motion separate the skin from the meat (9). Pull out any bones that are embedded in the meat with tweezers (10). If the fillet is particularly large, cut it in half lengthwise, following the backbone line in the fillet.

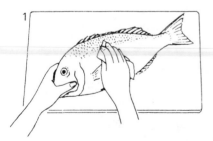

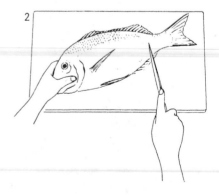

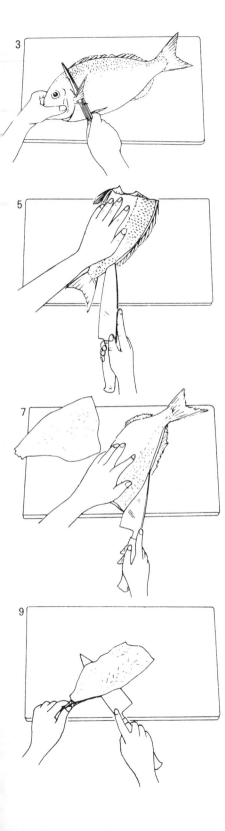

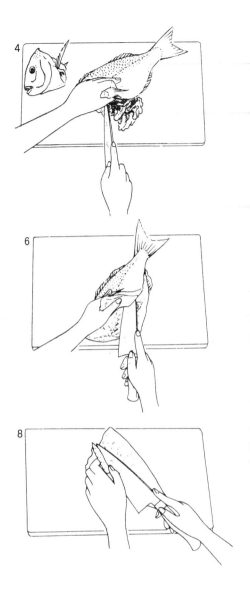

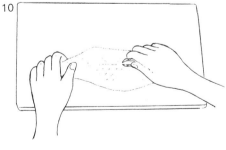

Five-part Method for Filleting Fish

Remove the head and entrails as in the three-part method. Place the fish on a cutting board so that the tail is facing you and make an incision along the center line from head to tail. Flip the fish over and repeat the process on the other side. Cut off the four fillets. Skin the fillets in the manner described for the three-part method.

When you are completed you will have the following: two sets of belly bones, two belly fillets, two back fillets, the spine with bones from the top side of the fish, and four pieces of *engawa*. Engawa is the name given to the meat that is found next to the side fins of a flatfish. The bigger the fish and the fins, the better the taste of the engawa. Only four pieces of engawa can be obtained from one flatfish. It is an excellent topping for finger sushi and is highly prized by sushi enthusiasts.

When buying shellfish, make sure they are more than fresh—make sure they are alive. This is a matter of some difficulty, seeing that most shellfish arrive in a shell and even if you could open them before buying, an old shellfish and a new one do not differ in color. Do not despair, for there are a few sure signs of freshness you can watch for: (1) shellfish should feel heavy when picked up, (2) shells should be tightly closed, (3) shells should be regularly shaped and uncracked, and (4) shellfish should not float—those that do are most certainly dead.

Compared with fish, shellfish live much longer after being caught. One need not worry too much about keeping them alive in water in the refrigerator. Just be careful to check the temperature in the refrigerator—if it dips too low the shellfish will die.

Japanese fishing boats ply the seas around the world in search of innumerable varieties of fish and shellfish. Returning to Japan, they lay out their catch at any one of the fish markets that are a feature of all the major seaports. The largest of these in Japan, and in the world, is at the Tokyo Central Wholesale Market, located in the Tsukiji district of the Japanese capital. An early-morning visit to this great bustling market (the auction starts at 5:40 AM) will attest to the efficient trolling and netting techniques developed by the Japanese fishing fleets. It will also give very graphic proof of the Japanese nation's voracious appetite for seafood. Add to this, a visit to one of the many small fish markets serviced by local fishermen, and it will be easy to understand why hundreds of lavishly illustrated pages are necessary to fully describe the fish and shellfish that are brought to market and find their way to restaurants and sushi shops in Japan.

What follows is a brief description of some of those fish and shellfish that are most commonly served as sushi in Japan. Where necessary, special preparation techniques are included. As was pointed out at the beginning of this section, only the freshest fish and shellfish are served as sushi. The information presented here can serve only as a guide. If you couple it with advice from your local fishmonger you should be able to select the best seasonal fish or shellfish.

Abalone (*Awabi*)

Finger sushi made with the meat of the abalone is a favorite of many sushi fans. The taste of most clams depreciates during the summer months, but not so the abalone. Hence it is doubly appreciated at that time of the year. Abalone cannot be eaten raw unless it is alive. If the meat contracts at the touch of your finger or seems to overflow its shell, you can be sure it is still alive.

The firmness of abalone meat differs according to its sex. The tougher meat of the male abalone is what you want to buy for making sushi.

To Prepare

Sprinkle the meat with a generous amount of salt. Scrub it vigorously with a stiff brush to get rid of any sliminess and foreign matter. Wash it in fresh water. Separate the meat from the shell by inserting a rice paddle or flat wooden spoon under the meat on the shallower side of the abalone and pry loose (1). Remove entrails with a knife (2). Wash the meat clean and cut it into thin slices.

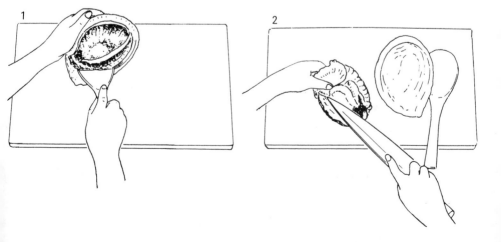

Ark Shell (*Akagai*)

Most mollusks are neutral in color, but not so the ark shell. Its distinctive vermilion color, due to a rich supply of hemoglobin in its blood, makes it an easy mark for the watchful shopper. A literal translation of the Japanese name for this mollusk is red shellfish.

The taste of ark shell is best from autumn to early spring. As spring turns into summer the taste of ark shell decreases in quality. Ark shell weighing about 100–220 grams are most suited for topping finger sushi. As is the case with most mollusks, it is best to prepare ark shell immediately before eating.

To Prepare

Wash the shell clean with a stiff brush. Insert the heel of a knife blade between the shell halves and pry open (1). Remove the adductor with your fingers (2). Be careful not to sever the threadlike filaments which connect the flesh to the shell. With the tip of a knife separate the filaments, called *himo*, from the meat (3–4). These filaments are also delicious eaten as finger sushi. Cut open the meat, scrape off the entrails with a knife. Cut away the thin membrane. Wash what remains in salted water.

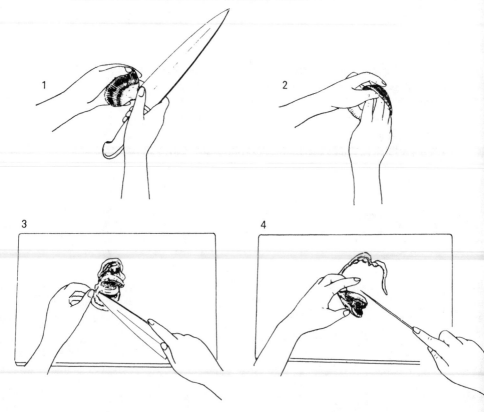

Cockle (*Torigai*)

The bivalve mollusk known as cockle is similar in shape to ark shell but it is a little wider across and thicker. It is also more finely ribbed. The brown and white triangular foot of this clam is an excellent ingredient for finger sushi. Live cockles are hardly ever seen in the market. Rather, cockles are shelled, and the foot cut, flattened, packed in a small box, and shipped out from where the cockles were gathered. When selecting cockles watch for the thicker meat; it is of better quality, but it is also more expensive.

To Prepare

Cockle meat can be used as it is for finger sushi. Before eating, wash it thoroughly in salted water. If you like, you can also brush the meat with a mixture of vinegar sweetened with sugar.

Conger Eel (*Anago*)

The Japanese *anago* eel is light brown in color and spotted. When buying conger eels, look for ones that are round and fat, with an underside tending toward yellow.

To Prepare

Place the fish on a cutting board, the head to the right and the back facing you. Pin the head down with a pointed instrument, inserting it between the eye and gills. Insert a knife through the back, just above the backbone, and laterally slice off the top fillet from head to tail (1–2). Carefully lift off the fillet and flip it over onto the cutting board. Cut through the backbone at the base of the head. Insert the knife blade underneath the backbone and, holding the

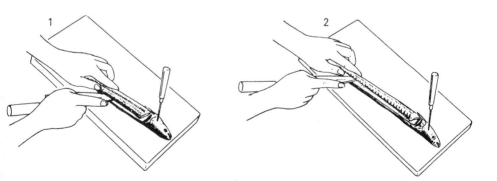

knife level, cut off the entire backbone from head to tail (3) and discard it. Remove the entrails. Cut off the dorsal fin. Scrape off the slimy skin film with the back of the knife. Rinse the fillets in water and drain. Season the conger eel fillets before eating.

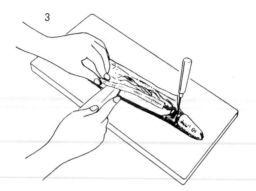

Seasoned Conger Eel

6–8 eel fillets
scant 1/2 cup sakè
scant 1/2 cup soy sauce
2 tablespoons mirin
2 tablespoons sugar

Combine sakè, soy sauce, mirin, and sugar in a saucepan and bring to a boil. Place the eel fillets, skin side down, in the boiling liquid. Continue to boil the liquid and fillets for 7–8 more minutes. A lid that fits inside the pan, directly over the fillets, will speed the process. Remove the fillets from the pan and cool. Grilling the fillets will further enhance their aroma.

A second method of seasoning eel fillets is called *shirani.* The manner of cooking is the same as that described above, but the ingredients differ. They are sugar, mirin, salt, and a very small amount of soy sauce, all in amounts determined by individual taste. This method produces paler colored and more delicately flavored fillets.

Eel (*Unagi*)

It is said in Japan that one who has mastered the art of dressing live eels is an expert cook. This is because the body of an eel is so extremely slippery. When considering eels for sushi, perhaps it is best to buy them dressed. If that is impossible, follow the directions for preparing conger eel.

When choosing an eel, be careful not to choose those that are too large, for these do not taste as good as smaller eels. The most savory are those weighing about 150 grams.

To Prepare

Cut the eel fillets into 2–3 pieces each. Pierce each piece with a skewer and grill. Grill the skin side first, then the meat side. Steam the grilled pieces (over strong heat) for about 5 minutes. Drain. Baste with a sauce of 3 parts mirin and 1 part sugar. Grill the pieces a second time, basting the pieces 2–3 times while grilling.

Fish Eggs

Fresh salted cod roe *(tarako)*, broken apart into separate eggs, goes well with sushi rice. Quality cod roe can be distinguished by its clear, reddish brown color, regular shape, and unpunctured membrane. Avoid vivid red cod roe because it most probably has been artificially colored.

Salted herring roe *(kazunoko)* is enjoyed on happy and auspicious occasions in Japan. In particular, it finds its way into the many special foods that are served over the New Year holidays. This is because the great number of eggs that form the roe augurs well for the birth of many children. Due to the dwindling catch of herring in recent years, the price of this delicacy has become prohibitively high, so much so that it has come to be called "yellow diamonds" in Japan. If you should spy some of these pale yellow eggs at the market and wish to serve them, look for eggs that are round and uniform in size. Small immature eggs and those that appear whitish in color are not nearly as tasty.

Before being eaten, herring roe should be desalted in water for at least two hours, changing the water from time to time. Priming the water with a little salt will speed the process.

An interesting and pretty variation of herring roe is called *ko-mochi kombu*. This is kelp on which herring have spawned their eggs. The pale yellow eggs that coat the dark green leaf of kombu is a delicacy popular with gourmets of Japanese cuisine. A short piece topping a finger of sushi rice is delicious. Like the roe that is taken directly from the fish, it must be desalted before eating.

The salted eggs of the salmon *(ikura)*, their ovarian membranes removed and unraveled, are delicious eaten as finger sushi.

It is said the Russians were the first to savor salmon roe. Connoisseurs of sturgeon roe, or caviar, it must have occured to them that the roe of the salmon might be just as delectable. The Japanese term for the roe of the salmon is derived from the Russian word *ikra* which means fish roe. Should the ovarian membrane remain intact, salmon roe is called *suzuko*.

Fresh salmon roe can be distinguished by its reddish color, luster, and smoothness. If it is left standing for any length of time, the eggs will turn whitish in color and the covering will wrinkle. It will regain its original shape and color if soaked in sakè for a short period of time.

Flat Shell (*Tairagai*)

Flat shell is triangular in shape. Its shell ranges from dark green to brown in color. As with scallops, only the adductor is eaten. Flat shells are packed and sold either whole and unshelled, or shelled.

To Prepare

Use a long-bladed knife. Insert the blade between the shell and the meat and sever the adductor. Repeat the operation on the other side of the meat and then remove the meat. As the adductor is quite large compared to the other parts, grip it while you remove the entrails that surround it. Remove the hard parts attached to the adductor. Peel off the thin membrane that covers the adductor. Wash the adductor clean in salted water. If you buy shelled flat shell, all you need do is peel off the adductor's membrane.

Flounder (*Hirame*)

One side of a flounder is light brown and speckled with milky white or beige spots and the other is white. The distinctive placement of the eyes on the brown side of the fish makes it easy to spot flounder at the fish market.

Flounder caught in the autumn is flavorful, but the best tasting fish are those caught in the winter. In Japan, the price of flounder fluctuates greatly, depending on where it is caught and how fresh it is.

Gizzard Shad (*Kohada*)

From early in Japan's history it has always been a common practice to change one's name as one progresses in one's profession.

Fish and shellfish: 1. sea bass, 2. mackerel, 3. sweetfish, 4. horse mackerel, 5. sea bream, 6. conger eel, 7. kuruma shrimp, 8. squid, 9. ark shell, 10. scallop, 11. abalone, 12. salmon roe, 13. herring roe, 14. sea urchin.

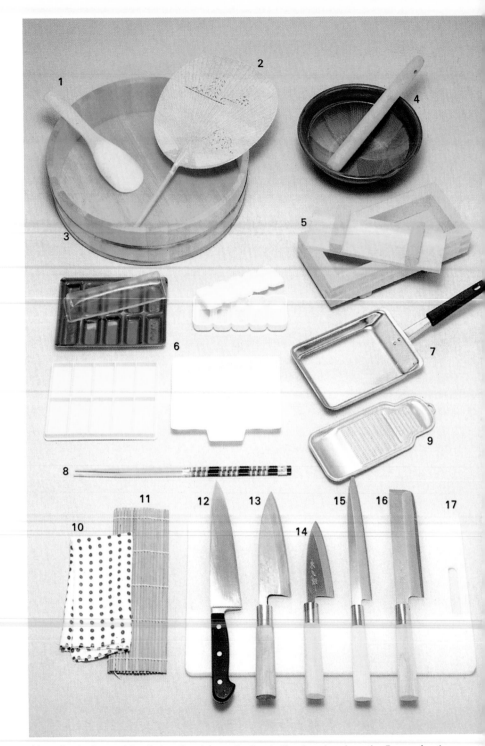

Utensils: 1. rice paddle, 2. fan, 3. mixing tub, 4. grinding bowl and pestle, 5. pressing box, 6. kit for forming finger sushi in bulk, 7. omelet pan, 8. cooking chopsticks, 9. grater, 10. cotton cloth, 11. bamboo rolling mat, 12. standard kitchen knife, 13–14. Japanese all-purpose knives, 15. Japanese fish knife, 16. Japanese vegetable knife, 17. cutting board.

Like the successful samurai, artist, or craftsman whose name has changed several times, so the name of the gizzard shad, or *kohada*, changes during its lifetime. In fact, it's not uncommon to hear kohada referred to as "success fish" in Japan. In addition to being called kohada, this fish, when it is at its best for sushi, is sometimes called *nakazumi* or *shinko*, and at maturity, *konoshiro*.

The spawning season of this fish is from the middle of March through June; during this time, its taste is at its worst. Autumn gizzard shad lacks fat and has a plain and simple taste that is preferred by some sushi devotees. From the end of December through February gizzard shad is most abundant. By then it has become rich in fat and its flavor has reached a second peak.

To Prepare

After filleting gizzard shad according to the three-part method, salt both sides of the fillets (about 1 tablespoon of salt to 4 fish) and allow to sit for 60–90 minutes. Wash off the salt, pat dry, and soak the fillets in a generous amount of vinegar for 5–10 minutes. Make 2–3 shallow slashes in the skin and use as desired.

Horse Clam (*Mirugai*)

A member of the round clam family, horse clam lives in a big shell from between which its long, chimneylike, muscular siphon reaches out of the ocean floor. It is the thick and crunchy siphon that is eaten as finger sushi. Other parts of the clam can also be eaten but their taste pales before that of the siphon. If the siphon meat of a horse clam is very firm and hard, you can be sure that it's fresh.

To Prepare

Pry open the shell with the heel of a knife. Pull out the meat and remove the entrails. Separate the siphon from the other parts. Wash the siphon in salted water to remove any sand. Pass the siphon through boiling water, allowing it to remain submerged for about 5 seconds. Skin the blackish surface and mouth of the siphon. (If the skin is hard to peel, it means the clam is all the fresher.) Insert a knife into the center part of the siphon. Cut it and spread it flat. Wash it a second time in salted water. Cut off the hard tip of the siphon. Now it's ready to be eaten. If you pass the skinned siphon meat a few times through boiling water it will turn red.

Mackerel (*Saba*)

Mackerel, a popular relative of tuna and bonito, is found in abundance in the waters around Japan. It is comparatively inexpensive and finds its way into many Japanese dishes. There are two species of mackerel, *ma saba* and *goma saba*. Autumn is the best season for ma saba and summer for goma saba; it is then that the meat becomes fatty and tasty. One drawback with either species of mackerel is that the fish easily loses its freshness. Mackerel meat that is less than fresh can cause one to have a nettle rash. Therefore, it is important that mackerel be prepared quickly, either by cooking or salting after removing the head and internal organs. After salting, the flesh, made taut with vinegar, has an exceptionally fine taste and texture.

Mantis Shrimp (*Shako*)

Related to the shrimp and crab, the mantis shrimp has a small head and chest and a flat back. Mantis shrimps average in length from 10 cm to 15 cm and are in season from May to June. When alive, the meat has a light grayish brown color, but once it is boiled, it changes to purplish red.

To Prepare

Mantis shrimps should be bought alive and boiled in salted water soon after purchasing. After boiling, the shell can be removed with scissors. Do not allow too much time to pass before eating boiled mantis shrimp, because once they are cooked it is very difficult to tell when the meat begins to spoil.

Octopus (*Tako*)

In Japan, octopus is an ingredient in several sushi dishes. Because the meat of the octopus is firm, it is very difficult to distinguish fresh from not-so-fresh meat. Therefore, if you plan to prepare octopus from scratch, take great care that you start with fresh octopus. Old octopus spoils very quickly and can become extremely toxic.

Fresh octopus can be distinguished by its pale gray color, frecklelike spots, and bouncy tentacles. When buying precooked octopus, see that the skin is not broken, that the ends of the tentacles are not blackish in color, and that the skin does not rupture when it is pulled. Avoid octopus that is a vivid red; it most probably has been artificially colored.

To Prepare

Remove the entrails located in the head. Cut out the eyes and beak. Rub the entire octopus with salt. Vigorously work the meat, from head to tentacle tips, with the salt, as if doing your laundry by hand. Be sure to clean out the suckers. Rinse the meat thoroughly with fresh water to remove all the salt and sliminess. Boil a generous amount of salted water. Gripping the head, slowly lower the octopus, tentacles first, into the boiling water. The length of time it takes to cook the octopus varies according to its size. Once the tentacles feel resilient you can assume that it is done. Remove it from the water and plunge it into cold water to cool. Slice the tentacles to the desired thickness.

Round Clam (*Aoyagi* or *Bakagai*)

The round clam is a bivalve shellfish with a very fragile shell. It is usually sold out of its shell, the meat being separated from the adductor. The meat is eaten raw if it is very fresh, that is, if it shrinks at the touch of a finger. After a quick wash in salted water it can be used just as it is for topping finger sushi. If it is only moderately fresh, the meat should be blanched for a few seconds and then immediately cooled in cold water before eating. Round clam is at its best in winter and spring. The muscle, called *kobashira*, is sold separately from the meat and is considered to be one of the best toppings for finger sushi. Cut into small pieces and served on top of vinegared rice that has had nori wrapped around the sides (page 66), the kobashira is soft in texture, with a light taste.

To Prepare

Squeeze the meat to push out the internal organs. Give the meat a good shake in cold water to rinse off any sand. Blanch for a few seconds, then cool in cold water and drain. Cut away the dark, jagged part at the edge and the mucous membrane. Cut down one side and open the meat halves flat, so that it will be easier to handle when making finger sushi. Remove any portion of the internal organs that should remain.

Scallop (*Hotategai*)

The adductor of the scallop makes very tasty finger sushi. Scallops can be bought alive in their shells or already shelled. In the latter case, make sure the meat is very firm as this assures you of its freshness.

To Prepare

Place the scallop on a cutting board with the flatter side down
and hinge on the far side. Insert a knife blade between the shell
halves and pry them apart. Insert the blade between the lower shell
and meat, being careful not to scar the meat, and cut the meat away
from the shell (1). Remove one half of the shell. Repeat this operation on the other side of the meat (2). Extract the meat with your hand.
Cut open the black section where the internal organs are located
and remove the entrails with your fingers (3). Wash the whitish
adductor clean in water and drain. Slice to desired thickness.

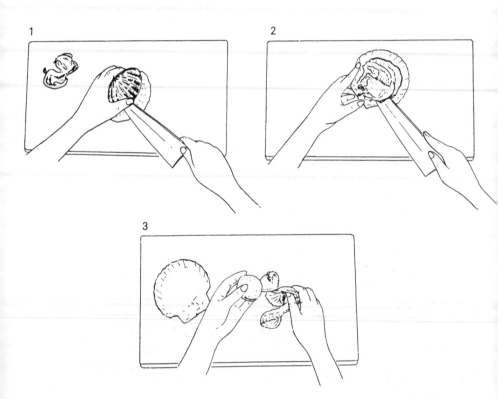

Sea Bass (*Suzuki*)

Like gizzard shad, the name of sea bass changes as the fish
matures, and so it, too, is called "success fish." When less than 25 cm
in length sea bass is called *seigo;* when about 40 cm long it is called
fukko; and only when it is fully grown and over 60 cm in length is
it called *suzuki.* These sizes and names may differ according to

where the fish is caught. Summer sea bass is the most tasty; winter sea bass, less so. The white meat of this fish is prized for its distinctive, subtle taste and is considered a delicacy.

Fresh sea bass is usually reserved for sushi or sashimi. Sea bass can also be broiled with salt or included in soup. When preparing small sea bass take care to preserve their particularly beautiful shape and color.

Sea Bream (*Tai*)

More than a hundred species of sea bream have been counted in the world. Some of the species which are savored in Japan are porgy (*ma-dai*), crimson sea bream (*chi-dai*), black porgy (*kuro-dai*), parrot fish (*ishi-dai*), and deep-sea porgy (*renko-dai*). Many are red in color. Sea bream retains its taste for a considerable length of time. Such is the Japanese respect for this fish that there is the saying *kusattemo tai* which means approximately the same as the Western expression "an old eagle is better than a young crow." Whole sea bream that has been tied with string into a curve, salted, and broiled is often the main course of a celebration dinner or is presented as a gift to celebrate a wedding or other congratulatory occasion. This is because the sound *tai* forms part of the word *omedetai* which means joyous or auspicious.

Besides being a delicious sushi ingredient, sea bream is also tasty when sautéed Western style in butter.

Sea Urchin (*Uni*)

The meat and eggs of the sea urchin is a sushi lover's delight. In its natural state, the sea urchin is enclosed in a thin brittle shell that is slightly flat and globular in shape and covered with sharp, movable spines that remind one of the prickly shell that encases a chestnut. Sold live, or shelled and steamed and packed in a shallow box, it is one of the tastiest ingredients for finger sushi. Fresh sea urchin can be distinguished by its vivid reddish orange color and smell. If you should have to choose from among many pieces, avoid those whose shape is not firm and those that have a watery look. The canned or bottled type of sea urchin, while delicious when eaten with other foods, is a poor second in taste when compared to fresh sea urchin.

The roe of the sea urchin is most often found at the market in a bottled form called *neri uni*. This also makes excellent sushi. A bottle of sea urchin paste will keep for a considerable length of time stored in the refrigerator.

Shrimp (*Ebi*)

Of all the many species of shrimp available around the world, the species called *kuruma ebi* in Japan has a taste and color particularly suited to eating as finger sushi. But, like all the very best ingredients, it is very expensive. The way to eat this shrimp is to dress and serve it alive, that is, still quivering with life. Should you have the opportunity to taste this delight you will understand why it is given the name *odori*, or dance.

Almost any live shrimp can be served in the odori fashion, but it is much more common to boil shrimp before dressing and serving them. A species of shrimp called *saimaki ebi*, which is about 5–6 cm long (minus the head), is a common sight at a sushi shop.

To Prepare

Wash the shrimps thoroughly. (If this is not done well, the color of the meat will turn.) Remove the back gut by inserting a toothpick between the joints in the shell (see illustration below). Thread with a skewer, on the leg side, through the head and down the tail. This will keep the shrimps from curling when they are boiled. Boil a generous amount of salted water. Drop in the skewered shrimps. Once the shrimps float, take them out and drop them into ice water. This will heighten their rosy color and make it easier to remove the skewers. It also helps to keep the shape of the shrimp. Drain. Remove the skewers, twisting as you pull. Shell and open the shrimps from the leg side. Remove the legs. Make a shallow incision along the leg side and flatten the shrimps. Devein the meat and press it flat. Refrigerate until ready to use.

Squid (*Ika*)

In the past only cooked squid was eaten as sushi or sashimi, but today's modern fishing techniques and freezing methods make it possible to enjoy the taste of raw squid.

To Prepare

Firmly grasp the tail with your left hand and grasp the tentacles at their base with your right hand and pull. The body will come apart and the tentacles and entrails will slip out of the body case (1). Carefully pull off the tail fins (2). Sprinkle salt on your hands to insure a good grip and carefully pull off the outer skin (3). Rinse off the case with water and dry.

1

2

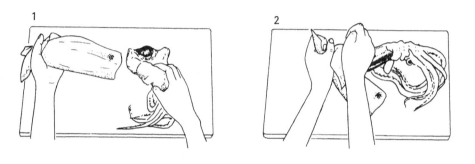

3

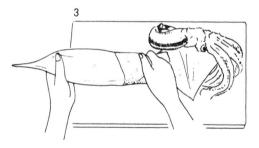

Tuna (*Maguro*)

There are several species of tuna, a large member of the mackerel family, that are found in the warm waters of the Atlantic and Pacific Oceans. In Japan, the best tasting species is called *kuro maguro* or *hon maguro.* It is caught from summer to winter, the period when the taste of its meat is at its best. Almost any part of the fish can be eaten raw. Other varieties are: bigeye tuna (*mebachi maguro*), albacore (*binnaga maguro*), and yellowfin tuna (*kihada maguro*). Bigeye and yellowfin tuna are eaten as sushi. Albacore consists almost entirely of very lean meat and, therefore, is not suitable for sushi. Instead, it is canned in oil.

The deep red lean meat, or *akami*, of the fish has only a small amount of lipid but the marbled underside of the tuna contains about 25% lipid and in some cases up to 40%. The marbled meat of the tuna is the tastiest—and the most expensive. There are three grades of fatty tuna meat: fatty (*toro*), medium fatty (*chu toro*), and very fatty (*otoro*). Each is distinguished by its pink color, very fatty meat being the whitest pink, and comes from a different part of the fish.

Yellowtail (*Hamachi* or *Buri*)

Like the gizzard shad and sea bass, the yellowtail also changes its name during its lifetime and is known as "success fish" in Japan. When it is young it is called *hamachi,* and when mature, *buri.* What is more, yellowtail goes by still other names depending on where it is caught. A relative of the horse mackerel family, yellowtail is a temperate-zone fish found in Japan's neighboring waters. Winter is the best season for mature yellowtail. The winter yellowtail eats great amounts of food to prepare for spawning in the spring. Once it fattens, its flesh becoming oily, it has an exceptionally good taste. Salted yellowtail is very popular in western Japan.

Utensils

The utensils you'll need to make sushi are probably already in your kitchen drawers and cabinets. Substitutes for those that are not handy can easily be devised. When making substitutes, two rules of thumb should be kept in mind. One, avoid metal utensils whenever possible. Vinegar is a major ingredient in all sushi dishes and should you prepare sushi with metal utensils the taste of the finished product will be adversely affected. Two, utensils of wood and bamboo should be new. Utensils made of these two materials tend to absorb odors and flavors from foods with which they come into contact. These odors and flavors can easily be transferred to raw fish, sushi rice, and fresh vegetables, making for unexpected and strange tastes.

Bamboo Rolling Mat (*Makisu* or *Sudare*)

A small mat made of extremely narrow strips of bamboo is used for rolling sheets of nori around rice and other ingredients to make rolled sushi. This mat comes in three sizes: large (the size of one whole sheet of nori) for making large rolls, and small (the size of half a sheet of nori) for making small rolls; the third, called an *oni sudare,* is made of thicker strips of bamboo and is used for shaping a rolled omelet. It is not necessary to purchase one of each of these mats. The large mat is the most versatile and can be used for the varieties of rolled sushi included in this book. Some of these recipes call for two mats, so it is recommended that you have two large mats on hand. A clean blind of bamboo strips, cut and tied to a manageable size, will suffice if precut rolling mats are not available in your area.

Chopsticks (*Hashi*)

Chopsticks come in various lengths, each according to how they are utilized. They can be made of unfinished or finished wood, lacquer, bamboo, or plastic. When collecting together the utensils for making sushi, be sure to acquire a single pair of long, wooden, cooking chopsticks called *saibashi*. They are about 25–30 cm in length, often feature a painted area at the handling end, and have a short string connecting the two ends. The string is for hanging the chopsticks and can be removed if you find it hampering when you use them.

Among the types of chopsticks used for eating *(ohashi,* but *otemoto* in sushi jargon) are a variety called *waribashi*. These are made of a single slat of unfinished wood which is nearly split lengthwise in two. Just before eating, waribashi are spread apart until they snap into two chopsticks. They are the easiest of all chopsticks to use for eating. Despite their pleasing appearance, plastic or lacquer chopsticks present problems for the novice, since their slippery surfaces make it difficult to grasp foods.

Cotton Cloth (*Fukin*)

A clean unbleached cotton cloth is used to prepare several varieties of sushi. Neither a dishcloth nor a table wiper can substitute for this cloth. If the cloth is new, wash it clean of starch and dry before use. It should not be too large; a square measuring 30 cm on each side is the easiest to handle. Since this cloth comes in direct contact with food, it should be kept clean and free of foreign matter at all times.

Cutting Board (*Manaita*)

A cutting board is essential for a variety of tasks. It is used when filleting, deboning, and slicing fish; as a cutting surface when preparing vegetables; and as a flat surface upon which nearly every type of sushi is made. A cutting board made of plastic or wood and about 24 × 40 cm in size will meet most if not all of your needs.

Because wood absorbs odors and flavors, a separate cutting board, identified with some kind of mark, should be set aside for usage with fish and shellfish. If you have a cutting board with both sides finished for cutting, reserve one side for using with fish.

Drainer (*Zaru*)

Great amounts of water are used when preparing Japanese food, so much so that Japanese cooking is sometimes referred to as "water cooking." Methods for draining off the water that is used to wash foods are many. The handiest method utilizes the bamboo draining basket called a *zaru*. Like so many other Japanese cooking utensils, these come in a variety of shapes and sizes, each suited to a particular task.

Plastic and metal drainers are also available but the bamboo drainer is most widely used because it is highly resistent to the effects of water, salt, and chemicals, and because it is easy to handle once it is soaked in water. Two disadvantages are that it tends to become moldy if not dried completely and aired after use and that it discolors with age. A plastic drainer may be colorful and dry quickly, but it is susceptible to heat damage and water easily clogs its holes. A wire drainer is very effective, but it might react with salt or other ingredients and impart a metallic taste to foods. An enamel-ware colander can be used to good effect for draining foods if you do not have a bamboo drainer.

Fan (*Uchiwa*)

A fan is necessary to cool hot rice while mixing it with vinegar dressing to make sushi rice. In Japan, an *uchiwa*, a round paper fan used to cool oneself on a hot summer day, is often used for this task. If a round paper fan is unavailable, an electric fan or a sheet of cardboard or plastic can be used in its place.

Grater (*Oroshi-gane*)

Any grater that is flat and has closely packed cutting teeth, whether it be made of copper, plastic, aluminum, stainless steel, ceramic, or whatever, can be used for the preparation of sushi. When purchasing a new grater be sure to select one that has very sharp teeth and is easy to handle. When using such a grater, especially when grating ginger root and wasabi, move your hand in a circular motion.

Grinding Bowl and Pestle (*Suribachi* and *Surikogi*)

A grinding bowl and pestle are used to pulverize fish and other ingredients. In Japan, an earthenware bowl scored on the inside surface and called a *suribachi* is used. A wooden pestle, or *surikogi*, is used with this bowl. Together they form a handy utensil useful in almost any type of cooking, Japanese or otherwise.

In the past, nearly all suribachi were made of earthenware, but at present one can also find plastic ones. Suribachi are available in many sizes, but one about 20 cm in diameter is sufficient for almost any grinding. A blender can be used to grind food when a suribachi and surikogi are unavailable.

Knives (*Hocho*)

Professional sushi chefs use a wide variety of knives, each suited to a particular purpose. For cooking at home, two or three types of knives are sufficient.

There are five knives used for making sushi in Japan. An all-purpose knife called a *banno-bocho* has become very popular among cooking enthusiasts because it can be used in many different ways. A large cleaver called a *deba-bocho* is used for chopping fish. Its weight makes it an excellent knife for lopping off the heads of fish or for cutting through bones. In fact, it is the thickest and heaviest of all Japanese kitchen knives. The *nakiri-bocho* is specially designed for cutting vegetables. Since olden days, this knife, with its wide, square tip, has been the most widely used in the home. The very thin, long-bladed *sashimi-bocho* is used for slicing boned fish fillets. It is the slimmest, the longest, and the sharpest of all kitchen knives. Most knives are used with a downward, pushing stroke, but when using a sashimi-bocho a pulling motion is preferred. If a soft and tender food such as fresh fish is sliced with a pushing motion, the meat is apt to fall apart, resulting in ragged cuts. The knife called a *sushikiri-bocho* is designed specially for sushi-making. The cutting edge of this knife is honed on both sides of the blade. It is used by professional sushi chefs and is hardly ever found in the home.

A knife used for making sushi must be kept sharp; a dull knife results in ragged cuts that detract not only from the appearance of the food but from its taste as well. Knives should be washed and thoroughly dried after each use.

When slicing sushi, the knife must be moist. A wet cloth neatly folded and placed beside your cutting board is an easy way to keep the blade moistened. It is also important to make certain that no foreign smell remains on the blade when slicing sushi. For example, do not use a knife that has just been used for cutting onions. This is true for almost any type of cooking, but it is particularly so when preparing sushi.

Mixing Tub (*Hangiri*)

In Japan, a large, flat-bottomed, wooden mixing tub, called a *hangiri,* is used for mixing cooked rice with the vinegar dressing. The wood serves to absorb excess moisture from the cooked rice, and the large mixing surface allows the hot rice to cool rapidly. A large mixing tub is better than a small one since, when making scattered sushi (page 83), for example, not only dressing and rice but other ingredients are mixed together in the tub. For making enough rice to serve three or four, a tub about 50 cm in diameter is required. A large, shallow tub (or bowl) that is resistant to the effects of acid and heat can be substituted for a hangiri. The shallower the tub the better, because rice that is cooled quickly and without too much stirring is much fluffier and better tasting.

Thoroughly wipe the inside of the tub with a clean cloth soaked in vinegared water before using. Unless the inside of the tub is moistened, rice will stick to its surface, making mixing difficult. After use, wash and dry the tub thoroughly.

Omelet Pan (*Tamago-yaki Nabe*)

A square-shaped frying pan about 3 cm deep, called a *tamago-yaki nabe,* is used exclusively for making several types of omelets. A thick iron pan that retains heat well makes the best omelet, but too heavy a pan is awkward to handle, so most cooks seem to prefer a thick pan made of aluminum. Although the shape of the omelet will differ, a conventional frying pan about 25–26 cm in diameter can be used in its place. This size or larger is preferred because the omelet that results will be large enough to be cut into a number of shapes.

Pressing Box (*Oshi-bako*)

A wooden pressing bix, called an *oshi-bako,* is indispensible for making box sushi. It consists of three parts—a pressing lid, a pressing frame, and a bottom. It is made of comparatively thick wood because it must withstand considerable pressure. Pressing boxes come in various sizes, but one with an interior 8 × 16 × 4 cm in size is sufficient in most cases. An empty cookie tin lined with waxed paper, or a layer-cake pan, can be used in place of a pressing box.

Rice Paddle (*Kijakushi* or *Shamoji*)

Some kind of flat and broad utensil is necessary to fluff, mix, and serve sushi rice. In Japan, a flat wooden paddle called a *kijakushi* or *shamoji* is commonly used. Shaped like a large, flattened spoon, this utensil is particularly suited for handling rice. While wood and bamboo paddles are the most common, lacquer as well as plastic ones are also found in kitchen utensil shops. A wooden paddle absorbs flavors easily, so it is best to set one aside especially for making sushi and to avoid those that have been used for frying or other types of cooking. If a proper Japanese rice paddle is not available in your area, a large wooden spoon will serve equally well.

Before using a rice paddle to scoop up hot rice or mix sushi rice, be sure to thoroughly moisten it. Otherwise, the rice will stick to the paddle.

Scaler (*Uroko Tori*)

A knife is sufficient to remove the scales from most fish, but for other fish such as sea bream and sea bass whose scales are more difficult to remove, a scaler is much more efficient.

Any standard fish scaler can be used for this task. It is used much like a knife is used for scaling. Simply draw it over the body of the fish, from tail to head, against the grain of the scales.

Skewers (*Kushi*)

Skewers are used when cooking certain fish, particularly shrimp and squid. They help to retain or improve the original shape of the fish or, in the case of shrimp and squid, to keep it from curling.

For cooking, either bamboo or metal skewers are used. These come in various shapes and lengths and are selected according to the fish that is to be skewered.

When pulling out the skewer, twist it as you pull. This frees the skewer from the meat and makes it easier to remove.

Sushi Rice

Nothing is more important to the sushi experience than the taste of sushi rice. Although it's possible to make sushi without fish, it's impossible to even imagine sushi without rice. Knowing this, it is no wonder that sushi shops spend such a great amount of time perfecting its taste and texture. The same amount of care is necessary when making sushi rice at home. Selecting the highest quality ingredients is the best way to start. To do this well, refer to the recommendations under *Ingredients and Basic Preparations.*

Once you've bought some good rice, the next problem is to cook it to perfection. It's not as difficult as you would expect, but it is an exacting process that once mastered will almost guarantee perfect rice. First, a proper pot.

Cooking Pot   A pot for cooking rice should have a snugly fitting lid and feature a bottom and walls that will evenly distribute heat. The size of the pot depends on how much rice you plan to make. Generally speaking, the more you cook the better the chances of ending up with delicious rice. Rice swells as it cooks, increasing anywhere from two and a half to three times in volume. A pot that will contain about 3–5 cups of cooked rice should be sufficient. If you own an automatic Japanese rice cooker, this makes everything easier. If you plan on doing a lot of Japanese cooking, a rice cooker is worth every cent as an investment. It will save you much time and many headaches.

Water   The amount of water necessary to cook rice depends on the kind of rice you are using. Too little will result in rice that is dry and hard in the center; too much will produce rice soup. As a rule of thumb, for cooking Japanese strains of rice grown in California about 20% more water than rice should give you good results. That means about 1 1/5 cups of water to 1 cup of dry rice. When cooking rice that was grown in Japan, 1 cup of *komai* (rice over a year old) is cooked with 1 cup or 1 cup plus about 1 1/2–2 tablespoons of water, and 1 cup of *shimmai* (newly harvested rice) is cooked with 1 cup or 1 cup minus about 1 1/2–2 tablespoons of water.

Rice One hour before you start cooking, wash the rice thoroughly in a flat-bottomed vessel, rubbing the wet grains against the bottom and sides. This will remove any bran or polishing compound that remains. Drain off the water and add fresh water. Repeat this step until the water becomes clear. Drain the rice, add water, and allow it to sit. No matter how much of a hurry you are in, wash the rice and soak it in water for at least 30 minutes before cooking.

Combine the rice and the measured amount of water in a saucepan and cover. Place the pan over moderately high heat. As soon as the water boils, reduce the heat and cook for about 10 minutes. Turn off the heat and allow the rice to steam undisturbed for at least 10 minutes. Do not remove the lid during the cooking process. The briefest peek will let out the steam and ruin the rice.

A tasty variation of this basic recipe is to cook the rice with kombu and sakè or mirin. When first heating the rice and water to cook three cups of dry rice, add a 6–7-cm-square piece of kombu (wiped beforehand with a damp cloth). Just as the water begins to boil remove the kombu and add one tablespoon of sakè or mirin for each cup of uncooked rice.

Vinegar Dressing While your rice is cooking or, better yet, before you put it on the stove, prepare the vinegar dressing for the rice. For 5 cups of dry rice combine in a bowl, stirring until clear:

7–8 tablespoons rice vinegar
1 tablespoon salt
4–5 tablespoons sugar (decrease by one-half if you are going to make finger sushi with the rice)

This is a good basic recipe. It will give you an excellent start on devising a recipe with different proportions that suits you own taste. The best way to start doing this is to adjust the amount of sugar. A dressing with too much sugar will not go well with finger sushi or other varieties of sushi that include raw fish. But box sushi, pressed sushi, and the like, which are eaten after they have been left standing for a considerable length of time, are made with a sweeter dressing. This is because the sugar in a sweeter dressing will help to keep the rice from becoming dry and flaky. Too much sugar, however, detracts from the refreshing taste of any sushi dish. Around Tokyo, sugar is used sparingly because most people who live there eat finger sushi and prefer a plainer tasting sushi rice that does not overpower the delicate, natural flavors of the fish and other ingredients used in this type of sushi.

Instant vinegar dressing is available at some stores that stock Japanese foods.

Mixing   Wet a large mixing tub with water. Wipe off any excess. Wet the tub a second time with vinegared water (1 cup of water with 2–3 tablespoons vinegar). Wipe off any excess. Heap the cooked rice in the center of the tub (1). Allow the rice to cool in the tub for about 10 minutes. Pour the vinegar dressing over the peak of the mound of rice (2). With a rice paddle or large wooden spoon, cut through the mound of rice to mix the dressing and rice evenly (3). As you mix, fan the rice to cool it (4). An extra hand will make this operation easier. Fanning the rice will give it a pearly luster. Brush off any rice that sticks to the side of the tub with a cloth dampened with vinegared water (5). Once the rice has cooled to body temperature it is ready to use.

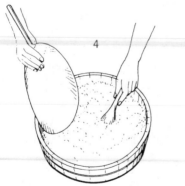

Varieties of finger sushi (p. 63): rolled omelet wrapped with a strip of nori, tuna, squid, shrimp, gizzard shad, sea urchin and lemon, sea bass, ark shell, and mantis shrimp. Pickled ginger slices (p. 12).

Top left: *rolled sushi with tuna (p. 70)*. Top right: *rolled sushi with conger eel and cucumber (p. 71)*. Center: *inside-out thick rolled sushi (p. 74), thick rolled sushi (p. 68), pickled ginger slices (p. 12)*. Bottom: *rolled sushi with mountain yam and takuan (p. 71)*.

Wisteria-shaped rolled sushi (p. 72). Pomegranate-shaped sushi (p. 81). Rolled sushi in comma shapes (p. 77), with pickled ginger stalks (p. 12).

Plum-blossom-shaped rolled sushi (p. 76). Coin-pattern rolled sushi (p. 80), with red-dyed ginger slices (p. 12). Four seas rolled sushi (p. 79).

Top: *box sushi made with shrimp (p. 89), box sushi made with eel (p. 92).* Bottom: *pressed sushi made with sea bream (p. 96), with pickled ginger slices (p. 12).*

Kansai-style scattered sushi (p. 84). Kanto-style scattered sushi (p. 83). Egg drop soup (p. 114).

ve-color scattered sushi (p. 85). Soup with bean curd and trefoil. Crab scattered sushi (p. 87).

Sushi rice and fish wrapped with a bamboo leaf (p. 105). Sushi rice topped with mackerel (p. 92). Steamed scattered sushi (p. 87), with nori strips.

Stuffed sweetfish sushi (p. 99), with pickled ginger stalks (p. 12). Sushi rice topped with strips of fish, omelet, and vegetables (p. 95).

Top, clockwise from top: *pine-cone-textured squid stuffed with sushi rice (p. 100), sushi rice in folded omelet (p. 103), sushi rice in gathered omelet (p. 102), stuffed squid sushi (p. 99).*
Bottom left: *devil's-tongue jelly stuffed with sushi rice (p. 105), with pickled ginger stalks (p. 12).*
Bottom right: *pouches of deep-fried bean curd stuffed with sushi rice (p. 104).*

Ingredients for making hand-rolled sushi (p. 98): sushi rice, nori, pitted umeboshi, coltsfoot, rolled omelet, conger eel, gizzard shad, mantis shrimp, shiso, tuna, sea bream, cucumber, squid, ginger root strips, shrimp, and wasabi.

Top: *varieties of finger sushi (p. 63), pickled ginger slices (p. 12)*. Bottom: *scattered sushi and rolled sushi arranged and decorated to resemble a cake (p. 107)*.

62

Finger Sushi

In Japan, the most popular type of sushi is finger sushi, or *nigiri-zushi*. A finger of sushi rice topped with a slice of fresh fish and a bit of wasabi is the easiest type of sushi to make. But, as with all things simple, special attention must be paid not only to the quality of the ingredients but also to their proportions and handling as well.

Finger sushi that seems to dissolve the moment it's put into your mouth is considered the best. To arrive at such finger sushi involves a careful balancing of several factors. The sushi rice must not be too sweet, the fish must be at its freshest (ideally, the final cuts should be made just before assembling), the cuts must be neither too thin nor too thick, and the wasabi should be freshly grated. These are things that a professional sushi chef working in a sushi shop considers in making finger sushi. When making finger sushi at home, keep in mind the following:

Rice Sushi rice prepared with a dressing a little less sweet than the recipe given earlier will be an excellent start on delicious finger sushi. Be careful that the rice is not too hot, otherwise it will impart an unpleasant warmth to the fish; if it's too cold, the grains will not adhere to one another. The temperature of the vinegared rice should match your body temperature. When forming a finger of rice, the trick is to make the outside just firm enough to be picked up with chopsticks or fingers without crumbling, yet loose enough so that it falls apart when put into the mouth.

Topping Nearly all species of fish and shellfish can top finger sushi. In an earlier chapter, brief descriptions and filleting instructions for some of the species of fish and shellfish that are served as finger sushi in Japan were given. In other parts of the world other species will be available. Saltwater fish are generally less prone than freshwater fish to spoil and to be carrying parasites. While it's best to cut fish just at the moment a finger of rice is ready to receive its topping, time does not allow one to do so when making finger sushi at home. Therefore, cut and neatly stack each type of fish you plan to use just prior to making finger sushi.

To slice fish fillets for topping finger sushi, first place the fillet horizontally on a cutting board so that the grain of the meat runs left and right. Place the tips of your left-hand fingers on the left end of the fillet. Measure off about 1 1/2 cm from the left end. With a long, sharp knife (a professional would use a sashimi-bocho) slice diagonally downward (1) and then draw the blade towards you to complete the cut (2). Pick up the slice of fillet and place it to the side. Continue slicing until you have enough to meet your needs.

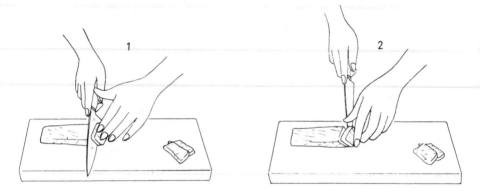

Wasabi   Wasabi that is freshly grated is the tastiest. If fresh is not available, powdered wasabi mixed with water or wasabi that comes in a tube can be used to give that special tang to a serving of finger sushi.

Vinegared Water   To facilitate shaping the rice and handling the topping for finger sushi, prepare ahead a bowl containing 1 cup of water acidulated with 2–3 tablespoons of vinegar. You'll be drenching your hands in this water so be sure to use a bowl that does not tip easily.

Assembly   The following is the basic method for making finger sushi used by professional sushi chefs. It is simple, deceptively simple. If you should find some of the operations difficult, do not hesitate to improvise your own method. The aim of this or any other method is to make appetizing finger sushi that will delight you, your family, and your guests.

Gather all your ingredients together. Since the temperature of sushi rice falls as you are making finger sushi, it is important to work fast. The only way to do that is to have everything ready and within easy reach before starting. Dip both hands into vinegared water making sure that every part that will come into contact with the rice and fish is thoroughly moistened (1). Form a portion of rice into a long, ovoid "finger" with your right hand against the side of the mixing tub. Pick up one piece of topping, in this case a piece of tuna, with the forefinger and thumb of your left hand. Handle it lightly to prevent the transfer of body heat to the fish (2). While holding the finger of rice with your last three fingers, spread wasabi on the inside surface of the fish with your right forefinger (3). Press the sushi rice against the fish with the right forefinger and middle finger. Press the rice with your left thumb from the side (4). Transfer

1

2

3

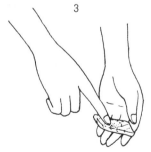

4

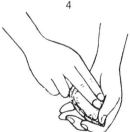

the rice and fish topping, fish side up, to your right hand (5).
Return the morsel to the left hand, flipping it over so that the rice
is on the bottom (6). Lightly squeeze the morsel with the right
thumb and forefinger into a pleasing shape (7). Give the fish topping
one last press to set it firmly on the rice.

Toppings that are extremely soft, composed of many small pieces,
or diced, such as sea urchin, fish roe, or certain shellfish, present
problems should you wish to serve them in the finger-sushi style.
But these are easily surmounted by wrapping a strip of nori
around the finger of rice. The finished product is called *gunkan maki,*
or battleship roll, because of its resemblence to a ship of war.

Place a flattened finger of rice on a clean, flat surface (1). Encircle
the rice with a strip of nori about 3–4 cm wide (2). Press the rice
down slightly and adjust the shape of the rice and nori (3). Fill the
hollow formed by the rice and nori with topping (4). Finger sushi is
illustrated in color on pages 51 and 62.

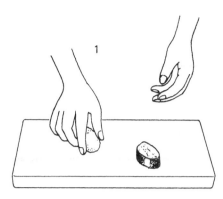

1

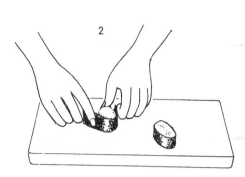

2

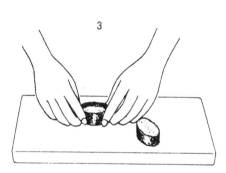

3

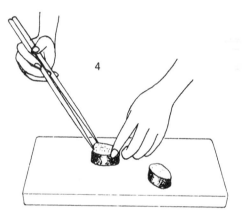

4

Rolled Sushi

After finger sushi the second most popular way of making sushi is a variation called *nori maki,* or rolled sushi. To make rolled sushi, sushi rice is first spread over a sheet of nori; fish and/or vegetables are laid in a line across the rice; and the nori, rice, and filling are rolled up together in a bamboo rolling mat. The long roll is then cut into bite-size pieces and arranged on a plate, cut side up, revealing their filling to the diner.

Many varieties of rolled sushi are filled with vegetables. Thus, it is an excellent way to treat your family and friends to sushi when fresh fish is unavailable.

Thick Rolled Sushi (*Futo-maki-zushi* or *Maki-zushi*)

The following recipe is one of the more common variations of this type of sushi. Almost any other filling material can be used in place of those listed.

4 rolls

2 1/2 cups uncooked rice, prepared as for sushi rice
4 sheets nori
4 rolled omelets (page 9), cut into 1-cm-square strips
4 40-cm long strips of seasoned kampyo (page 13), cut as long as
   the nori sheets are wide
4 seasoned shiitake (page 19)
1 piece seasoned freeze-dried bean curd (page 5), cut into 1-cm-
   square strips
10 grams of spinach or trefoil leaves, cooked in salted water, soaked
   in cold water, and squeezed dry
vinegared water (1 cup water with 2–3 tablespoons vinegar)

Place a sheet of nori, horizontally and front side down, on a rolling mat (1). Wet your hands with vinegared water and scoop up about a quarter of the sushi rice and spread it evenly from left to right over the nori (2), leaving about 3–4 cm of the far edge of the nori uncovered. Make a low ridge of rice at the far end of the area covered with rice (3). This ridge will keep the ingredients from shifting position. Arrange a quarter of the omelet, kampyo, shiitake, spinach, and bean curd strips just in front of the ridge (4). Pick up the end of the rolling mat and the nori (5). Roll everything together in the direction of the ridge, stopping when you reach the ridge (6). Adjust the form of the roll by squeezing it gently. Finish rolling, making sure that the end of the sheet of nori sticks to the roll to seal it. Allow a few minutes for the roll to set. Carefully

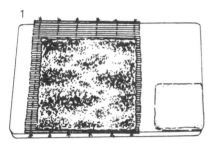

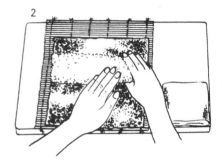

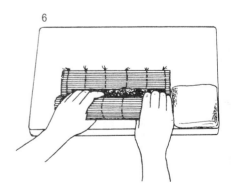

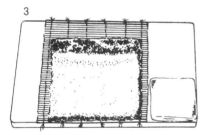

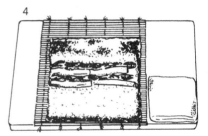

remove the mat. Moisten a knife with a wet cloth (7). Cut the roll into eight pieces (8). Thick Rolled Sushi is illustrated on page 52.

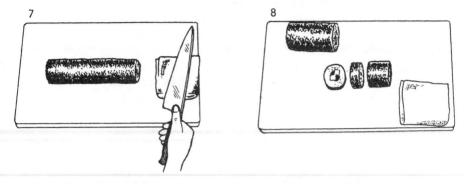

Narrow Rolled Sushi (*Hoso-maki-zushi*)

With this variety of rolled sushi, almost any number of fillings can be enjoyed with a minimum of ingredients. Compared with Thick Rolled Sushi, Narrow Rolled Sushi is much smaller and easier to eat.

When making this variety of rolled sushi, it is important to use the proper amount of rice. Too much rice results in holes in the nori. To be on the safe side, too little rice is better than too much. As a rule of thumb, for one roll use about 1 1/2 balls of rice the size of an egg.

The method for assembling and rolling Narrow Rolled Sushi is the same as that for Thick Rolled Sushi except that less rice is used and only half a sheet of nori is necessary for wrapping the roll. To cut the sheet of nori use a pair of kitchen shears and cut on the line perpendicular to the fold in the sheet.

Recipes for four standard varieties of this type of sushi follow. In addition, sea urchin, umeboshi, takuan, natto, herring roe, or cod roe are also delicious rolled up in sushi rice and nori. Several varieties of Narrow Rolled Sushi are illustrated on page 52.

Narrow Rolled Sushi with Tuna (*Tekka Maki*)

2 rolls

1 scant cup uncooked rice, prepared as for sushi rice
1 sheet nori, cut in half
2 8-cm square strips of tuna, cut as long as the nori is wide
wasabi

Before placing the strip of tuna in front of the ridge of rice, spread a line of wasabi along the bottom of the ridge with your finger. For variations, add chopped green onions, chives, or ginger root strips.

Narrow Rolled Sushi with Cucumber (*Kappa Maki*)

In Japanese folklore, a *kappa* is a water imp with a hollow in the top of its head which must always be filled with water for the kappa to keep its strength. Nothing delights a kappa more than a feast of cucumbers, hence the name of this variety of rolled sushi.

2 rolls

1 scant cup uncooked rice, prepared as for sushi rice
1/2 cucumber, sliced lengthwise into long, narrow strips
wasabi

Narrow Rolled Sushi with Conger Eel (*Anago Maki*)

2 rolls

1 scant cup uncooked rice, prepared as for sushi rice
2 seasoned conger eel fillets (page 30)
1/2 cucumber, sliced lengthwise into long, narrow strips

Narrow Rolled Sushi with Mountain Yam (*Yamaimo Maki*)

2 rolls

1 scant cup uncooked rice, prepared as for sushi rice
50 grams mountain yam, peeled and soaked in vinegared water for
    about 20 minutes and cut into narrow strips
60 grams takuan, cut into long, narrow strips
bonito shavings
soy sauce

Place the yam and takuan strips on the rice and sprinkle with bonito shavings seasoned with soy sauce.

Wisteria-shaped Rolled Sushi (*Fuji no Hana-zushi*)

The gracefully trailing blossoms of the wisteria vine, a familiar sight in Japan during the months of May and June, are the inspiration for this very decorative sushi presentation. As this type of sushi comes in easy-to-eat pieces it works particularly well as an hors d'oeuvre. It is quite simple to make and doesn't take too many ingredients. Depending on how much you make, wisteria sushi can be a whole meal in itself; it can also make an elegant centerpiece for a party table.

2 sprays

1 2/3 cups uncooked rice, prepared as for sushi rice
2 sheets nori, cut in half
150 grams fresh salmon meat
1 egg
1/2 teaspoon salt
1 teaspoon sugar
1 teaspoon cooking oil
vinegared water (1 cup water with 2–3 tablespoons vinegar)

Pink-tinted Sushi Rice   Boil the salmon in salted water and remove any skin and bones. Break up the meat into very small pieces or flakes with a fork or chopsticks, or grind it in a grinding bowl.
Place the ground salmon meat in a small saucepan, add the salt and sugar, and, stirring constantly, cook over low heat for 3–4 minutes or until the meat becomes dry and fluffy. Transfer it to a small bowl. Mix the sweetened and parched meat with half of the sushi rice and set aside.
Yellow-tinted Sushi Rice   Beat the egg together with a pinch each of salt and sugar. Pour into a small frying pan greased with cooking oil and scramble the eggs until they are dry. (The smaller the pieces of egg the better.) Finely mince the eggs. Mix the egg with the remaining sushi rice.
    Place a half-sheet of nori horizontally on a rolling mat. Wet your hands with vinegared water. Spread half of the yellow-tinted rice over the central area of nori leaving about 1 cm of the two long edges of the nori uncovered (1). With the rolling mat, fold the nori over the rice to make a teardroplike shape (2). Repeat this procedure with the remaining tinted rice and nori, making a total of four rolls. Place one roll of yellow-tinted rice and one roll of pink-tinted rice on

a cutting board, their seams facing away from you. Moisten the blade of a knife on a wet cloth and slice the two rolls in half at one time (3). Place the four pieces together. Moisten the knife again and slice all four rolls in half again (4). Line up the eight pieces, moisten the knife blade, and slice them in half again. Lift the blade quickly so the rice adhering to the knife blade serves to lift the cut sides up to reveal the alternating pink and yellow teardrop shapes (5). Arrange the pieces in a slight curve on a large serving platter or tray, reserving one piece for the bottom of each wisteria spray. Repeat the process with the remaining two rolls. Wisteria-shaped Rolled Sushi is illustrated in color on page 53.

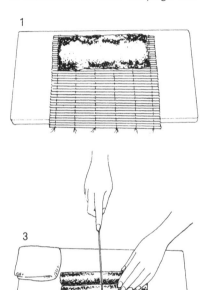

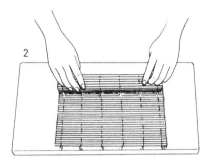

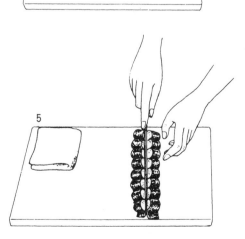

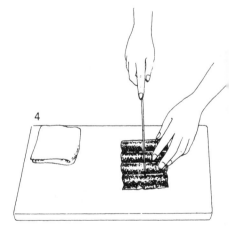

Inside-out Thick Rolled Sushi
(*Kawari Futo-maki-zushi*)

This variety of rolled sushi is made of two layers of sushi rice separated by a sheet of nori. When rolled and cut, the finished product features a spiral of nori on its face. This roll is larger than Thick Rolled Sushi. If you are short of nori, this recipe will help you to stretch it and still enjoy a meal of sushi.

2 rolls

1 2/3 cups uncooked rice, prepared as for sushi rice
1 sheet nori, cut in half
1 rolled omelet (page 9), cut into narrow strips
1/2 cucumber, sliced lengthwise into long, narrow strips
2 seasoned shiitake (page 19), sliced into strips
1 tablespoon black sesame seeds
vinegared water (1 cup water with 2–3 tablespoons vinegar)

Divide the rice into four parts. Place a sheet of nori vertically on a rolling mat. Wet your hands with vinegared water and spread one part of the rice from left to right over the entire sheet of nori (1). Place a moistened cloth over a second rolling mat. Lay the rice-covered nori, rice side down, on the cloth (2). Wet your hands with vinegared water and spread another part of the rice over the nori (3). On the edge closest to you place one-half of the strips of omelet and mushroom and some long strips of cucumber (4). Roll up the towel, rice, and ingredients in the mat as you would for Thick Rolled Sushi (page 68). Press the roll to set it and adjust its shape (5). Unroll the mat and carefully remove the towel. Lift the roll and place it on a cutting board. To garnish, sprinkle some black sesame seeds in a a line along the roll (6). Wrap the roll in clear plastic wrap that has been moistened with vinegared water (7). Cut into two, four, and then eight pieces (8). Repeat the procedure to make a second roll.

For a variation, substitute a sheet of oboro kombu for the plastic wrap. Inside-out Thick Rolled Sushi is illustrated in color on page 52.

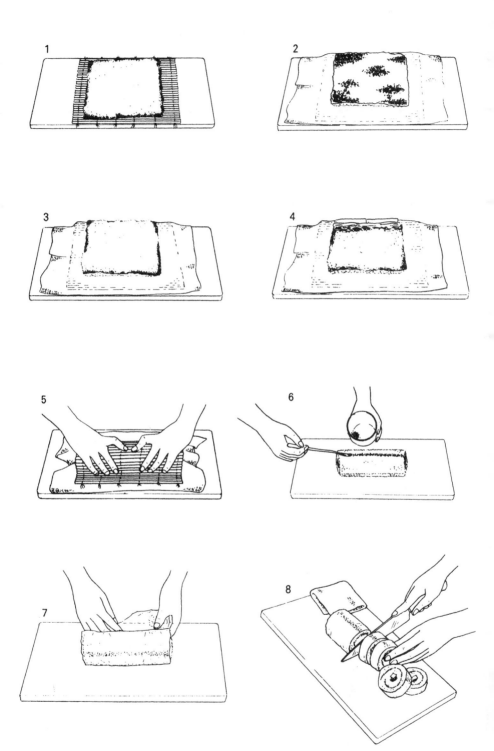

Plum-Blossom-shaped Rolled Sushi (*Umebachi Maki*)

This decorative sushi is used to add an accent of color and variety to an artistic arrangement of several types of sushi.

2 rolls

1 scant cup uncooked rice, prepared as for sushi rice and divided into ten portions
1 sheet nori, cut in half
2 1/2 sheets of nori, cut into quarters (The half-sheet is simply cut in half, thus making a total of 10 quarter-sheets.)
2 1-cm-square strips of rolled omelet (page 9) about 10 cm long or 2 wieners, boiled and cooled
vinegared water (1 cup water with 2–3 tablespoons vinegar)

Place a quarter-sheet of nori horizontally on a rolling mat. Wet your hands with vinegared water. Spread one portion of rice over the nori leaving the far edge of the nori uncovered (1). Roll the rice and nori with a rolling mat (2). Repeat the process with the remaining rice and quarter-sheets of nori, making a total of ten rolls. Place a half-sheet of nori vertically on the rolling mat (3). Lay three rolls of rice on the half-sheet. On top of the center roll place a strip of omelet or 1 cooked wiener (4). Lay two rolls on top of the egg or wiener and secure the bundle together with the half-sheet of nori. To secure the half-sheet slightly moisten the overlapping edge with a damp cloth (5). Cut in half and then in quarters. Standing each piece on end will reveal the five-petaled plum blossom with a colored center from which this type of sushi takes its name (6). Repeat the process with the remaining five rolls and half-sheet of nori. Plum-Blossom-shaped Rolled Sushi is illustrated in color on page 54.

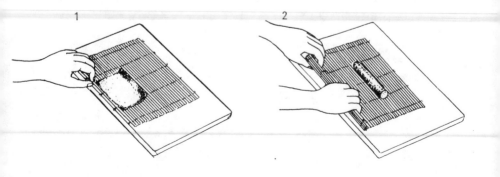

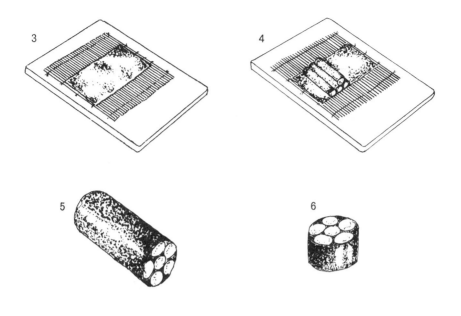

Rolled Sushi in Comma Shapes (*Tomoe-zushi*)

A circle made of two interlocking comma shapes, called a *tomoe*
in Japan, is a design motif found throughout the world. In Japan,
it is used as a family crest or as a decorative device on the ends of
roof tiles or on other objects. The type of sushi that incorporates this
motif is relatively difficult to make. Before inviting guests to applaud
your skill at making this variety of sushi, it would be prudent to have
a dress rehearsal.

2 rolls

1 scant cup uncooked rice, prepared as for sushi rice
2 sheets nori, 1 sheet cut widthwise into thirds
40 cm seasoned kampyo (page 13)
1 piece seasoned freeze-dried bean curd (page 5), cut into
    1-cm-square strips
100 grams spinach, boiled in salted water, rinsed in cold water, and
    squeezed dry
vinegared water (1 cup water with 2–3 tablespoons vinegar)

77

Place a sheet of nori vertically on a rolling mat. Wet your hands with vinegared water and spread one half of the sushi rice over the sheet (1) in such a way that by the time you reach two-thirds of the way up the nori the layer of rice is very thin. Lay half the kampyo, bean curd strips, and spinach on the rice about one-third of the distance from the top of the incline (2). Roll the mat over the nori, rice, and filling (3). Add a third-sheet of nori over the exposed nori and rice at the end of the roll, aligning the two far edges (4). Correct any irregularities in the comma shape by tapping the ends of the roll and manipulating the rolling mat (5). Remove the roll from the mat and cut it in half. Replace one-half of the roll in the rolling mat (6). Rest the other half inside the first, its "head" within the "tail" of the first. Roll the two halves together with the rolling mat (7). Adjust the shape and allow the roll to set for a moment. Remove the roll from the mat. Moisten a knife on a wet cloth and quarter the roll (8), thus revealing the interlocking comma shapes. Repeat the process to make a second roll. Rolled Sushi in Comma Shapes is illustrated in color on page 53.

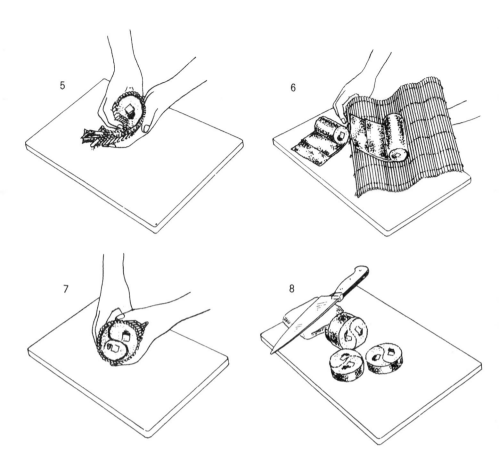

Four Seas Rolled Sushi (*Shikai Maki*)

2 rolls

1 scant cup uncooked rice, prepared as for sushi rice
3 sheets nori. Cut 1 sheet in half; 1 sheet in quarters; and 1 sheet in
 half, and each half cut once again along a line that marks 1/3 of
 the half-sheet's length (see illustration on next page)
2 1-cm-square strips of rolled omelet (page 9), cut the same
 length as a half-sheet of nori
vinegared water (1 cup water with 2–3 tablespoons vinegar)

Place one of the smallest sheets of nori horizontally on a rolling
mat. Wet your hands with vinegared water. Spread a small amount

of rice on the nori and roll into a slim roll (1). Place a quarter-sheet of nori horizontally on the rolling mat. Wet your hands with vinegared water. Spread with rice and place the just-made slim roll on the center of the rice (2). Roll the two together, the slim roll centered within the larger roll (3). Place a third-sheet of nori horizontally on the rolling mat. Wet your hands with vinegared water. Spread with rice and place the double roll just made in the center (4). Roll to form a still larger roll (5). Cut the three-part roll in quarters lengthwise (6–7). Arrange the quarters, their cut sides out, around the strip of omelet and wrap with a half-sheet of nori to make a square bar. Adjust the shape and allow to set for a few moments. Slice into quarters. Repeat this procedure to make a second roll. Four Seas Rolled Sushi is illustrated in color on page 54.

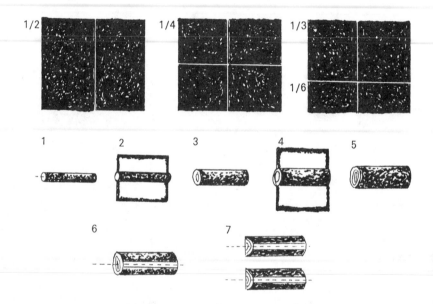

Coin-pattern Rolled Sushi (*Bunsen Maki*)

This is a variation of Four Seas Rolled Sushi (page 79) in which the pattern created by the dark-colored nori and white rice is similar to the pattern seen on a medieval Japanese coin and an abstraction of one of the two ideograms used to write the name of the coin in Japanese. The ingredients are identical except that two three-part rolls are utilized to make one very large, round roll.

Cut the two three-part rolls in half lengthwise. Place a half-sheet of nori vertically on a rolling mat. Arrange the halves, their cut sides out, around the strip of omelet. Roll the bundle in the half-sheet of nori. Allow to set for a few moments. Carefully remove the mat and slice into quarters. Coin-pattern Rolled Sushi is illustrated in color on page 54.

Pomegranate-shaped Sushi (*Zakuro-zushi*)

The bright red orange salmon roe "seeds" against the dark nori "skin" of this sushi pomegranate are a delight to the eye. While the recipe that follows makes 10 large "fruits," simply adjusting the sizes of the nori and omelets you can make bite-size "fruits" which are especially good with sakè.

10 "fruits"

1 2/3 cups uncooked rice, prepared as for sushi rice and divided
    into ten portions
10 thin omelets (page 8), cut into 13-cm squares
10 sheets nori, cut into 15-cm squares
3–4 tablespoons fresh salmon roe, herring roe, or cod roe
vinegared water (1 cup water with 2–3 tablespoons
    vinegar)

On a square of nori center one of the omelets. Roll one portion of rice into a ball (1). Lay a nearly dry, damp towel over your left hand. Place the nori and omelet on the towel. In the center rest the ball of rice (2). If the towel is not sufficiently wrung out, the nori will

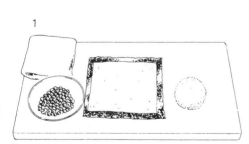

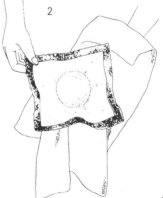

become damp and maybe even stick to the towel. Gather the towel up around the nori, omelet, and rice and form a ball, gently gathering the towel underneath (3). Correct the shape. Carefully unfurl the towel and remove the nori-covered rice ball. Moisten the blade of a knife on a wet cloth and slash a cross in the top of the ball (4). If you have lots of roe on hand, make the slashes deep. Carefully turn back the nori and omelet skin and stuff the roe into the opening (5). Pomegranate-shaped Sushi is illustrated in color on page 53.

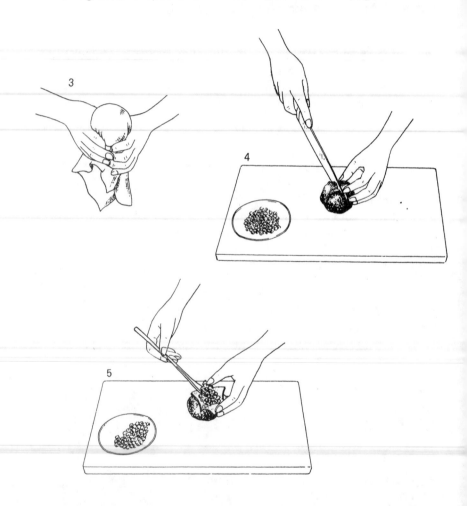

Scattered Sushi

The easiest of all sushi to prepare is a saladlike dish called *chirashi-zushi*, or scattered sushi. It resembles nothing so much as a Western rice salad and can be served at any time of the year, to guests or to family. In some districts of Japan this dish is called *gomoku-zushi* or *bara-zushi*. Whatever its name, the taste experience is unique, wherever you eat it. Indeed, there are as many variations of scattered sushi as there are people who make it, and it's not too much to say that almost any vegetable, cooked or fresh, or fish, grilled or raw, has at sometime or other been incorporated into this dish.

Introduced here are five representative variations of scattered sushi, one of which is steamed. Once you've made any one of these dishes you can immediately begin to explore other possible combinations of ingredients. Improvisation is the key to delicious scattered sushi. Making do with what's on hand in your kitchen will surely reveal some surprising taste experiences. Giving a new concoction an artistic and appetizing name will add even more to your fun.

Kanto-style Scattered Sushi (*Kanto-fu Chirashi-zushi*)

Just as the name of this dish suggests, this type of scattered sushi is popular in Kanto, the area in and around Tokyo.

4 servings

2 1/2 cups uncooked rice, prepared as for sushi rice
20 grams seasoned kampyo (page 13), chopped into small pieces
4 shrimps. Devein, boil in salted water, shell, and sprinkle with 2 teaspoons of vinegar sweetened with 1/2 teaspoon sugar.
2 seasoned conger eel fillets (page 30), cut into bite-size pieces
1 gizzard shad, 150 grams fresh tuna, and 150 grams fresh squid.

Cut each into bite-size pieces and sprinkle with sweetened vinegar as for the shrimps.

1 2-egg rolled omelet (page 9), cut into 1-cm cubes

4 seasoned shiitake (page 19), cut into bite-size pieces

50 grams lotus root. Peel, slice thin, and soak in vinegared water for 10 minutes. In a saucepan boil enough water to cover the slices. Add a pinch of salt and a dash of vinegar. Add the slices and boil for 30–40 seconds. Remove the slices from the water and marinate for 10 minutes in a mixture of 2 tablespoons stock no. 2 (page 6) or water, 1/2 teaspoon salt, and 1 teaspoon sugar.

1 cucumber. Sprinkle with salt, roll on cutting board to soften, slice thin, and remove seeds.

pickled ginger slices (page 12), or wasabi

Mix the kampyo with the sushi rice. Place the rice mixture in a large serving dish and arrange the remaining ingredients on top. Garnish with pickled ginger slices or wasabi.

To serve, scoop up rice along with the topping. Do not mix the ingredients in the large serving bowl. This will destroy the decorative effect and make the rice mushy. Kanto-style Scattered Sushi is illustrated in color on page 56.

Kansai-style Scattered Sushi
(*Kansai-fu Chirashi-zushi*)

This is the kind of scattered sushi commonly served in Kansai, the area around Osaka and Kyoto.

4 servings

2 1/2 cups uncooked rice, prepared as for sushi rice

4 seasoned shiitake (page 19), cut into bite-size pieces

10 grams seasoned kampyo (page 13), cut into small pieces

1–2 pieces seasoned freeze-dried bean curd (page 5), cut into thin 1-cm squares

100 grams bamboo shoots. Slice into thin 1-cm squares and season over moderate heat in a saucepan containing a scant 1/2 cup stock no. 2 (page 6), 1/2 teaspoon salt, 1 teaspoon mirin, 1 teaspoon soy sauce, and a pinch of salt.

4 seasoned conger eel fillets (page 30), cut into bite-size pieces

50 grams lotus root, prepared as for Kanto-style Scattered Sushi
(page 83)
50 grams green beans, boiled in salted water and chopped into
small pieces
1 2-egg thin omelet (page 8), sliced into narrow strips
1 sheet nori, cut in half and then into narrow strips
pink-dyed ginger strips (page 12)

Mix the rice with the shiitake, bean curd, bamboo shoots, eel, kampyo,
and ginger strips. Place the rice mixture in individual serving bowls.
Arrange the beans, egg strips, and lotus root slices on top of each
serving. Sprinkle with nori strips just before serving. Kansai-style
Scattered Sushi is illustrated in color on page 56.

Five-color Sushi (*Goshiki-zushi*)

4 servings

2 1/2 cups uncooked rice, prepared as for sushi rice
200–250 grams minced white chicken meat. Fry the meat in an
ungreased frying pan until well cooked. Remove the pan from the
heat. Push the cooked meat to one side and remove any excess
fat. Add 2 tablespoons sugar, 1 tablespoon mirin, and 3 tablespoons soy sauce. Return the pan to the heat and cook the meat
until it is dry.
4–5 eggs. Beat together with 1/2 teaspoon salt and 1 teaspoon sugar.
Scramble the eggs in a greased frying pan over low heat, stirring
vigorously to make the pieces of egg very small. (Stirring with a
bundle of 7 or more chopsticks will give excellent results.)
200 grams carrot. Peel and slice into narrow strips. Sprinkle with 1/3
teaspoon salt and gently knead with hands until strips are limp.
Rinse and squeeze dry. Marinate in 1 teaspoon vinegar.
3–4 bell peppers. Boil until soft. Remove from water before their
color changes. Slice into narrow strips and drain.
200 grams white fish meat (frozen flounder or salmon, canned
salmon, or canned tuna can be substituted). Boil the fish in lightly
salted water with 2–3 thin slices of ginger root that have been
minced. Remove the skin and bones and transfer the fish to a grinding bowl. Add 1 1/2–2 tablespoons sugar and 1/2 teaspoon salt
and pulverize the mixture in a grinding bowl. If you don't have a

grinding bowl, finely mince the meat and mix with salt and sugar. Parch the mixture over low heat until all the moisture evaporates. As the grinding of fish meat is a time-consuming task, it is recommended that you make this preparation in bulk and keep it in the refrigerator for future use.

50 grams ginger root. Peel and slice into short strips. Soak in water for 5 minutes and drain.

2 tablespoons white sesame seeds, roasted to a golden brown

Fill a large serving dish with rice. Sprinkle the sesame seeds and ginger over the rice. Visually divide the surface of the rice into five equal areas. (This is easiest to do in a round dish.) In each area place one of the prepared toppings: chicken meat, egg, carrot, peppers, and fish.

The chrysanthemum garnish shown in the color illustration on page 57 is made with a thin omelet. Prepare a thin omelet (page 8). Fold the omelet into thirds, placing two sides over the center (1). Fold this folded omelet in half again (2). With a sharp knife make cuts into the open side of the long, narrow, folded omelet at about 5-mm intervals, cutting halfway across the omelet (3). Gently roll the omelet from the end (4). Separate the loops to open the "chrysanthemum" (5). Place 2–3 clean chrysanthemum leaves in the center of the dish of rice and set the omelet chrysanthemum in the center.

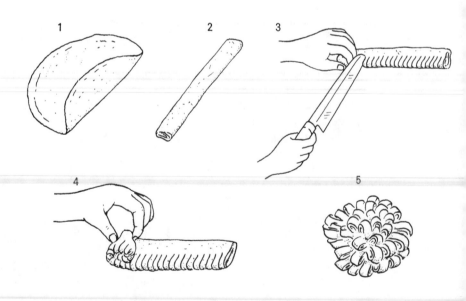

Scattered Sushi with Crab (*Kani Chirashi-zushi*)

4 servings

2 1/2 cups uncooked rice, prepared as for sushi rice
180–200 grams crab meat, shredded (frozen or canned crab will do)
  and sprinkled with 1 tablespoon lemon juice
2–3 eggs made into thin omelets (page 8), cut into strips
1–2 cucumbers. Wash and slice thin. Sprinkle with 1/3–1/2
  teaspoon salt and knead. Wash in fresh water and squeeze dry.
50 grams lotus root, prepared as for Kanto-style Scattered Sushi
  (page 83)
2 large seasoned shiitake (page 19), cut into strips

Simply mix all the ingredients together in a large serving dish and
serve. Using small shrimps in place of the crab meat makes for a tasty
variation of this dish.
  Scattered Sushi with Crab is illustrated in color on page 57.

Steamed Sushi (*Mushi-zushi*)

Piping hot, steamed sushi is a delicious dish to serve on a cold
winter day. Since it is so good, it's recommended that you make
more than you need. Not only will you wish you had made more
once you have tasted this dish, it is also one of the few sushi dishes
that can be kept in the refrigerator for a day or two. Any leftover
that remains can be resteamed and served a second time.

4 servings

2 1/2 cups uncooked rice, prepared as for sushi rice
10 grams seasoned kampyo (page 13), cut into small pieces
4–5 seasoned shiitake (page 19), diced
1 piece seasoned freeze-dried bean curd (page 5), diced
2 seasoned conger eel fillets (page 30), cut into bite-size pieces
4 shrimps. Devein, boil in salted water, and shell.
2 eggs made into thin omelets (page 8), cut into strips
50 grams green beans, boiled in salted water and cut on the
  diagonal into bite-size pieces
1 sheet nori, cut in half and then into narrow strips

Combine the rice, kampyo, shiitake, and bean curd and place in a heat-resistant bowl, or covered casserole. (Small individual serving bowls that are heat-resistant can also be used.) Lay the pieces of eel and the shrimps on top of the rice mixture. Steam for 13–15 minutes. Remove from the heat. Arrange the omelet strips and green beans on top and serve. Place the nori strips in a separate bowl and have them available for people to sprinkle on their sushi just before eating. Steamed Sushi is illustrated in color on page 58.

Box Sushi and Pressed Sushi

With the three-piece pressing box (or suitable substitute) or by simply pressing sushi rice and toppings together you can easily make the many interesting and delicious types of sushi known as *hako-zushi* and *oshi-zushi*, or box sushi and pressed sushi. The recipes that follow tell you how to make three varieties of this type of sushi. Once you have tried your hand at one of these, concoct your own variations.

Whenever making pressed sushi, once you have removed it from the pressing box frame wait a few minutes before cutting the finished product. This will allow the individual flavors of the ingredients to blend.

Shrimp Box Sushi (*Ebi no Hako-zushi*)

8 × 16 × 4 cm pressing box

1 scant cup uncooked rice, prepared as for sushi rice
5 shrimps, each 8–10 cm long. Remove the back gut. Skewer and boil in salted water until the color changes. Soak immediately in cold water. Remove the legs and shells. Soak in a marinade of 2 tablespoons rice vinegar, 2 tablespoons stock no. 2. (page 6), 1 tablespoon mirin, 1 1/2 teaspoons sugar, and 1/3 teaspoon salt for 5–10 minutes. Slash each shrimp along its underside and spread flat.
2 seasoned shiitake (page 19), cut into strips
1/2 teaspoon wasabi
bamboo leaves, or aspidistra leaves, aluminum foil, or plastic wrap
vinegared water (1 cup water with 2–3 tablespoons vinegar)

Moisten the three parts of the pressing box with vinegared water. Lay leaves, or substitute, on the bottom of the pressing box (1).

Lay enough of the shrimps, back side down, to cover the bottom of the box. Alternate the direction of the shrimps to ensure complete coverage (2). With your finger spread wasabi evenly over the shrimp. Wet your hands with vinegared water. Spread one-half of the rice over the shrimps (3). Sprinkle the shiitake strips over the rice (4). Wet your hands with vinegared water. Spread the remaining half of the rice over the shiitake (5). Lay leaves, or substitute, over the rice (6). Moisten the pressing box lid in vinegared water and place on top of the leaves (7). Press down on the lid evenly, changing hand positions several times to ensure an even press. Remove the side frame with the fingers while the lid is secured with the thumbs (8). Remove the lid and the layer of leaves (9). Flip over the stacked ingredients. Remove the box bottom and layer of leaves (10). Moisten a knife blade on a wet cloth and slice. Transfer to a serving dish. Serve with soy sauce. Shrimp Box Sushi is illustrated in color on page 55.

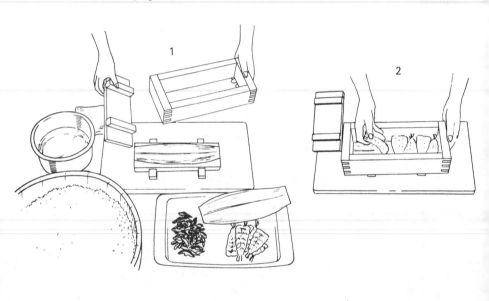

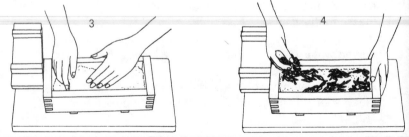

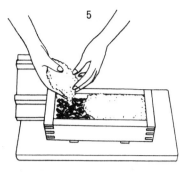

5

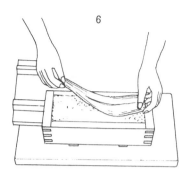

6

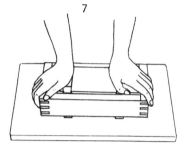

7

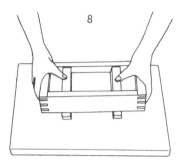

8

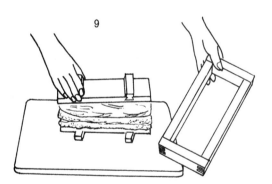

9

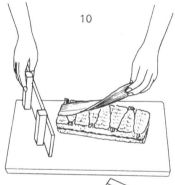

10

Conger Eel Box Sushi (*Anago no Hako-zushi*)

8 × 16 × 4 cm pressing box

1 scant cup uncooked rice, prepared as for sushi rice
4 seasoned conger eel fillets (page 30). While still warm, flatten
    fillets with a heavy spoon or spatula and cut to fit pressing box.
1 cucumber. Thinly slice and soak in 1 scant cup of water containing
    1 teaspoon salt. Once limp, remove slices from the salted water
    and squeeze dry.
20 grams ginger root, peeled, cut into narrow strips, and soaked in
    water
bamboo leaves, or aspidistra leaves, aluminum foil, or plastic wrap
glaze: mix and boil 1 teaspoon each of soy sauce, mirin, and sugar
vinegared water (1 cup water with 2–3 tablespoons vinegar)

Assemble as for Shrimp Box Sushi (page 89) in the following order:
leaves, or substitute; eel pieces, skin side up; ginger strips; half of
the sushi rice; cucumber slices; remaining sushi rice; and leaves.
Before cutting, brush eel pieces with glaze. Conger Eel Box Sushi is
illustrated in color on page 55.

Mackerel Stick Sushi (*Saba no Bo-zushi*)

2 sticks

1 2/3 cups uncooked rice, prepared as for sushi rice
1 medium-size mackerel. Dress according to three-part method.
    Salt both sides of the fillets generously and allow to set for at
    least 4 hours. (This salting can be done a day ahead.) Wash the
    fillets and pat dry. Marinate in 1/2 cup vinegar sweetened with
    2 tablespoons sugar for 30–60 minutes. (The length of time is
    variable according to taste.)
50 grams ginger root, peeled and cut into narrow strips
vinegared water (1 cup water with 2–3 tablespoons vinegar)
optional: 30-cm length of shiraita kombu. Boil for approximately
    3 minutes in 2 tablespoons vinegar, 1/2 tablespoon sugar, 2
    tablespoons water, and a pinch of salt. Remove and drain.

Mix the ginger strips and rice. Set aside. Remove the bones from the marinated mackerel fillets, using tweezers if necessary (1). Pull off the thin outer skin starting from the head end of the fillets (2). Be careful not to pull off the silvery blue underskin which is beautiful as well as edible. Laterally slice the fillet in half (3). Soak a cotton cloth in vinegared water and wring dry. Place it on a rolling mat (4). Place fillet slices, skin side down, on the cloth and mat. Make sure the slices are flat. Add smaller pieces of meat to the sides to form a rectangle (5). Wet your hands with vinegared water. Spread half of the rice and ginger mixture over the fish (6). Roll

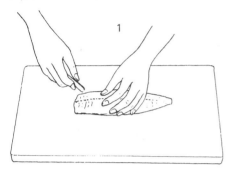

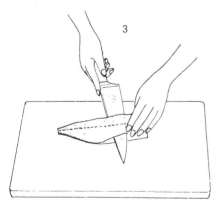

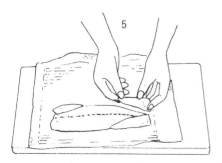

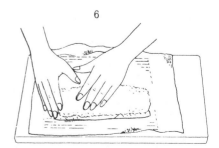

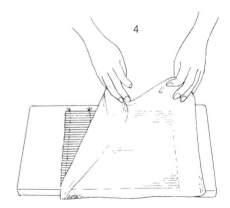

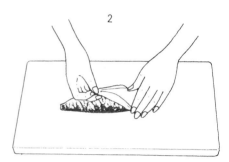

the mat and cloth over the rice and fish (7) and press slightly. Turn the roll over so that the fish is on the top. Apply pressure to the mat to adjust the shape (8). Allow to set for a few moments. Carefully lift the mat and cloth away from the fish and rice. Lay a piece of shiraita kombu (or plastic wrap) over the fish (9). Cut into 8 equal pieces and serve. Repeat this procedure to make a second stick. The shiraita kombu can be eaten with the sushi but the plastic wrap will, of course, have to be removed. Mackerel Stick Sushi is illustrated in color on page 58.

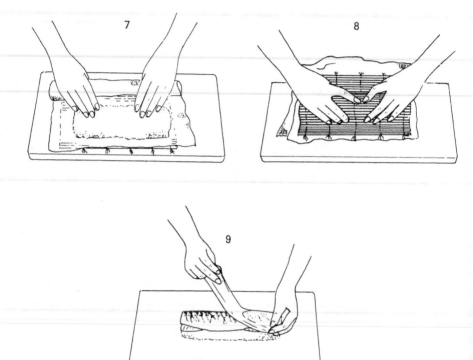

Barber Pole Sushi (*Tazuna-zushi*)

Tazuna refers to a type of decoration composed of alternating diagonal stripes of two contrasting colors, most often red and white. This decoration resembles the stripes on a candy cane or a barber-shop pole. This recipe incorporates many differently colored ingredients, but a simpler variation could incorporate only two differently colored ingredients and have the same decorative effect.

2 rolls

1 scant cup uncooked rice, prepared as for sushi rice
2 sheets of nori
50 grams squid, prepared as for Stuffed Squid Sushi (page 99) and
    cut into 1 × 5 cm strips
2 shrimps, each about 7–8 cm long, prepared as for Shrimp Box
    Sushi (page 89)
1 1-egg rolled omelet (page 9), cut into 1-cm square strips
small amount of mackerel, or other silver-skinned fish such as
    gizzard shad, prepared as for Mackerel Stick Sushi (page 92) and
    cut into 1 × 5 cm strips
5-cm-long piece of cucumber. Sprinkle with salt. Roll on a flat
    surface to soften. Cut into 1-cm square strips
vinegared water (1 cup water with 2–3 tablespoons vinegar)

Soak a cotton cloth in vinegared water and wring dry. Place on a rolling mat. Arrange, in a slanted row, the sliced squid, shrimp, fish, omelet strips, and cucumber, upside-down on the cloth (1). Cut one sheet of nori to fit the row of fish, omelet, and vegetables and lay it over the back of this row of ingredients (2). Wet your hands

1

2

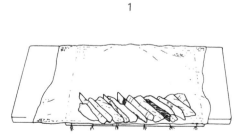

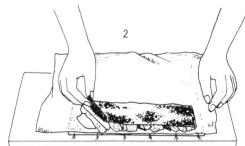

with vinegared water and spread half of the rice over the nori (3). Roll the cloth and rolling mat over the rice and toppings (4). Press down slightly. Roll the ingredients together (5). Adjust the shape of the roll and allow to set for a moment. Carefully remove the mat and cloth (6). Repeat this procedure to make a second stick. Slice and serve with soy sauce. Barber Pole Sushi is illustrated in color on page 59.

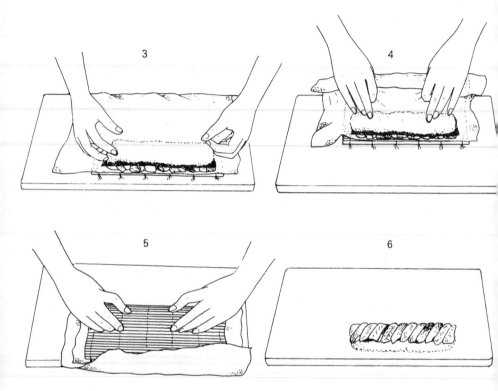

Sea Bream Pressed Sushi (*Shime-dai no Oshi-zushi*)

2 bars

- **1 2/3 cups uncooked rice,** prepared as for sushi rice
- **1 300-gram sea bream.** Fillet according to three-part method. Sprinkle evenly with 2 tablespoons salt and allow to sit for 30–40 minutes. Wash and tap fillets dry. Marinate for 10–20 minutes in 1/2 cup rice vinegar sweetened with 1 tablespoon sugar. (The fillets will discolor if marinated for too long.) Pull out any small

bones with tweezers and cut the fillets lengthwise in two. Laterally slice the fillets so that all pieces are equal in thickness to the belly meat.

vinegared water (1 cup water with 2–3 tablespoons vinegar)

Lay a damp cotton cloth over a rolling mat. Arrange the fish slices, skin side down, in the center of the cloth in a row about 6–7 cm wide. Wet your hands with vinegared water. Lay the rice on top of the fish. Roll the cloth and rolling mat over the rice and fish and squeeze gently. Turn the mat over so that the fish is on top. Apply pressure to the mat to adjust the shape. Allow to sit for a few minutes. Carefully remove the mat and slice.

If this dish is prepared ahead of time, it's recommended that you wrap the completed roll in shiraita kombu or plastic wrap, otherwise the flavor will deteriorate and the rice will dry out. Any leftover marinated fish can be served as finger sushi. Sea Bream Pressed Sushi is illustrated in color on page 55.

Miscellaneous Sushi Varieties

Hand-rolled Sushi (*Temaki-zushi*)

Perhaps the easiest way to share a sushi experience with friends is to serve them *temaki-zushi*, or hand-rolled, do-it-yourself sushi. All you need to do is to prepare ingredients in advance, attractively arrange them on plates or a large tray, and encourage your guests to experiment. To hand roll your own sushi, spoon some sushi rice on a small piece of nori, add a pinch of wasabi or strips of ginger, and then roll it up with a bit of fish and some vegetable strips.

Almost anything that would go well with the tastes of sushi rice and nori can be included in hand-rolled sushi. Strips of cooked chicken, ham, sausage, and even rare roast beef make delicious fillings. The list of ingredients that follows will give you an idea of how much to prepare for a gathering of four people. Hand-rolled Sushi is illustrated in color on page 61.

2 1/2 cups rice, prepared as for sushi rice
10–12 sheets of nori, cut into quarters
8 shrimps, each about 8–10 cm long. Devein, skewer, and boil in
    salted water. Shell and cool.
4 seasoned conger eel fillets (page 30), cut into pieces as long as
    a quarter-sheet of nori
150–200 grams each of fresh squid, tuna, or other fish, cut into
    strips as long as a quarter-sheet of nori
1 2-egg rolled omelet (page 9), cut into strips as long as a quarter-
    sheet of nori
2 cucumbers. Peel and salt and rub on a clean, flat surface. Slice
    into narrow strips as long as a quarter-sheet of nori.
150 grams *fuki* (coltsfoot), generously salted. (If canned, simply
    blanch and transfer to serving dish. If fresh, boil in salted water,
    then plunge into cold water. Remove the outer skin in the cold
    water.) Cut into pieces the length of a quarter-sheet of nori.

80–100 grams ginger root. Cut into needlelike strips. Soak in cold water and drain.
wasabi

Stuffed Sweetfish Sushi (*Ayu no Sugata-zushi*)

4 servings

1 1/4 cups uncooked rice, prepared as for sushi rice
4 sweetfish, or small trout. Being careful not to destroy their shape, scale and gut each fish, and wash well. With the point of a knife cut each fish in half through the lower jaw along the belly and all the way to the base of the tail. Spread the fishes open and remove the bones. Sprinkle both sides of each fish with a mixture of 1 1/4 cups vinegar sweetened with 1 tablespoon sugar. (Do not overmarinate because the taste of this fish is particularly delicate.)
pickled ginger stalks (page 12)
vinegared water (1 cup water with 2–3 tablespoons vinegar)

Soak a cloth in the vinegared water and wring dry. Place it on a cutting board. Wet your hands with vinegared water. Scoop up a quarter of the sushi rice and place it on the cloth in approximately the shape of the fish. Place one of the fish, opened side down, on the rice and gently shape it around the rice. Pick up the edge of the cloth and lay it over the fish. Roll the fish with the rice. Arrange on a serving dish, adjust the tails, and garnish with pickled ginger stalks. Stuffed Sweetfish Sushi is illustrated in color on page 59.

Stuffed Squid Sushi (*Ika no Sugata-zushi*)

4 servings

1 1/4–1 2/3 cups uncooked rice, prepared as for sushi rice
4 medium-size squid, dressed. Boil the squid in salted water for about 20 seconds and drain. Cut the tentacles and side fins into small pieces and cook for 10 minutes in a scant 1/2 cup stock no. 2 (page 6), 1 tablespoon mirin, 1 tablespoon soy sauce, and 1 teaspoon sugar. Allow to cool.

1/2 cucumber. Peel and thinly slice. Sprinkle with 1/3 teaspoon salt and knead until cucumber slices are limp. Rinse and drain.
1 tablespoon sesame seeds, roasted to a golden brown
vinegared water (1 cup water with 2–3 tablespoons vinegar)

Mix the small pieces of cooked squid, cucumber slices, and sesame seeds with the rice. Wet your hands with vinegared water. Stuff the four squid bodies with the rice mixture and slice into bite-size pieces. Serve with wasabi or grated fresh ginger and soy sauce. Stuffed Squid Sushi is illustrated in color on page 60.

Pine Cone Sushi (*Matsukasa-zushi*)

2 rolls

1 1/4 cups uncooked rice, prepared as for sushi rice
2 medium-size squids, dressed
2 10-cm-square sheets of nori
40 cm of seasoned kampyo (page 13), cut to match the length of the squid body
2 seasoned shiitake (page 19), cut into strips
2 tablespoons white fish meat, prepared as for Five-color Sushi (page 85)
20 grams snow peas, boiled in salted water and cut into narrow strips
vinegared water (1 cup water with 2–3 tablespoons vinegar)

Cut the squid along the belly (1). Spread it flat on a cutting board. Holding your knife at a slant, crosshatch one side of the squid meat with shallow slashes about 5 mm apart (2–4). This will prevent the meat from curling when cooked and give it a texture reminiscent of a pine cone. Bring a saucepan of salted water to a boil, drop in the slashed squid meat and allow it to cook for about 15 seconds. Remove the squid, drain, and let cool (5). Place the cooled squid meat, slashed side down, on the cutting board. Wipe off any water that remains. Lay a sheet of nori on the squid meat, fitting it inside the curved edges (6). Wet your hands with vinegared water. Spread half of the rice on the nori. With your finger make a shallow furrow lengthwise in the center of the rice. Place half of the kampyo (7), shiitake, fish, and snow peas in the furrow. Set aside. Place a rolling mat on the cutting board; cover with a damp cotton cloth. Place the filled squid meat on the cloth and roll in the cloth and rolling mat (8).

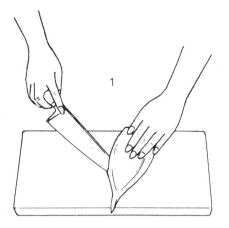

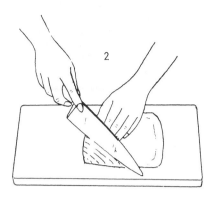

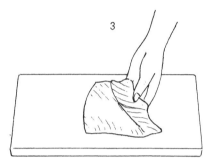

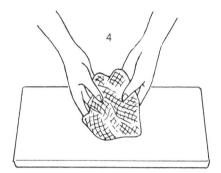

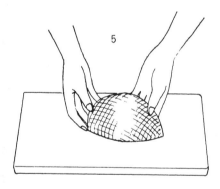

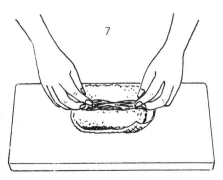

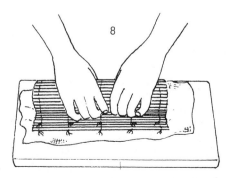

Adjust the shape. Carefully unroll the mat and cloth and place the rolled squid on the cutting board (9). Slice to desired thickness. Serve as is or garnish with wasabi or pickled ginger slices and serve with soy sauce. Pine Cone Sushi is illustrated in color on page 60.

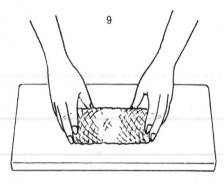

Tea Cloth Sushi (*Chakin-zushi*)

8 pieces

1 1/4 cups uncooked rice, prepared as for sushi rice
100 grams bamboo shoots. Cut the shoots into thin 5-cm squares.
    Cook in a scant 1/2 cup stock no. 2 (page 6), 1 teaspoon
    sugar, 1 teaspoon soy sauce, and a pinch of salt.
2 large, seasoned shiitake (page 19), cut into strips
8 thin omelets, cut into 16–17-cm squares
8 long spinach leaves, blanched in salted water
8 small shrimps. Boil in salted water, shell, and devein.
1 tablespoon sesame seeds, roasted to a golden brown
vinegared water (1 cup water with 2–3 tablespoons vinegar)

Mix bamboo shoots, shiitake, and sesame seeds into the sushi rice. Divide the rice into 8 portions. Wet your hands with vinegared water. Place one portion of rice in the center of an omelet square. Gather up the corners of the omelet and tie it up in a bag shape, using a spinach leaf as a string (1). With your thumb, press down the corners that stick up, thereby flattening the shape so it will sit well (2). Garnish with a shrimp. Tea Cloth Sushi is illustrated in color on page 60.

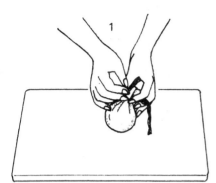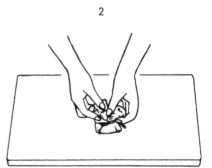

Silk Square Sushi (*Fukusa-zushi*)

8 pieces

Mix ingredients as for Tea Cloth Sushi (preceding page). Shape one portion of rice into an ovoid and lay it at an angle in the center of an omelet square. Fold the corners of the omelet over the rice (1). Tie up the folded corners with a spinach leaf (2). Garnish with a shrimp. Silk Square Sushi is illustrated in color on page 60.

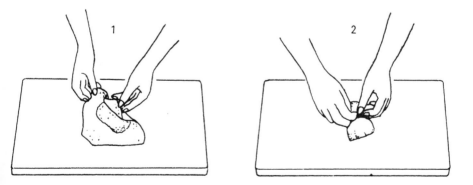

Fox Sushi (*Inari-zushi*)

The fox appears in many guises in Japanese folklore. A most mis-
chievous animal, it is often playing tricks on humans. The fox is also,
however, the messenger of Inari, the god of the harvest, with whom
the fox is identified. As one of the fox's favorite foods is deep-fried
bean curd slices, the sushi made with it is called *Inari-zushi*.

The recipe that follows includes many ingredients to be added to
sushi rice that is then stuffed into seasoned pouches made of deep-
fried bean curd slices. Like most sushi recipes, this list can be
abbreviated or substitutes can be used as you see fit. Some people
add nothing to the rice; others, only sesame seeds.

24 pieces

2 1/2 cups uncooked rice, prepared as for sushi rice
12 pieces of deep-fried bean curd. Cut in half and open into
   pouches. (If difficult to open, roll each piece with a rolling pin.
   This will make separation easy.) Boil for about 1 minute to rid
   pieces of excess oil. Drain. Combine 1 1/4 cups stock no. 2
   (page 6), 5–6 tablespoons sugar, and 3–4 tablespoons soy sauce
   in a saucepan. Add salt to taste. Bring to a boil over high heat.
   Lay in the pieces of deep-fried bean curd and boil until the liquid
   evaporates. Be careful not to puncture them while cooking.
   Remove the pieces from the pan and drain.
100 grams carrot. Cut into narrow strips. Sprinkle with salt and
   knead until limp. Wash and squeeze dry.
100 grams burdock. Cut into narrow strips and soak in vinegared
   water for a few minutes. Boil in stock no. 2 until soft. Cook a
   second time in 1 tablespoon soy sauce, 2 teaspoons sugar, and 1
   teaspoon mirin until liquid evaporates.
3–4 seasoned shiitake (page 19), cut into narrow strips
100 grams snow peas, boiled in salted water and cut at an angle
   into small pieces
2 tablespoons white sesame seeds, roasted to a golden brown
vinegared water (1 cup water with 2–3 tablespoons vinegar)

Mix carrot, burdock, shiitake, snow peas, and sesame seeds with
sushi rice. Stuff into seasoned pouches. For variety, some of the
pouches can be turned inside out or cut on the diagonal to make
small triangles. Fox Sushi is illustrated in color on page 60.

Devil's-Tongue-Jelly Sushi (*Konnyaku-zushi*)

16 pieces

1 2/3 cups uncooked rice, prepared as for sushi rice
2 8 × 15 × 4-cm cakes of devil's-tongue jelly. Cut the jelly
   widthwise in half and then cut each half in half diagonally to make 8
   triangular pieces. Sprinkle pieces with salt, knead, and boil in
   water for 5 minutes. Cut the pieces laterally in half to make 16
   equally shaped triangular pieces. Make a slash into the longest
   side of each triangle. (Make it deep enough to allow you to stuff
   the piece.) Boil the pieces for 10 minutes in 1 1/4 cups stock no.
   2 (page 6), 2 1/2 tablespoons sugar, 4 1/2 teaspoons soy
   sauce, and 1 1/2 teaspoons salt. Cool.
100 grams carrot. Cut into narrow strips, sprinkle with salt, and
   knead until limp. Wash and squeeze dry. Sprinkle with 1/2
   teaspoon vinegar.
30 grams snow peas, boiled in salted water and cut into narrow
   strips
1 tablespoon white sesame seeds, roasted to a golden brown
2 large, seasoned shiitake (page 19), cut into narrow strips

Combine carrots, snow peas, shiitake, and sesame seeds with sushi
rice. Stuff each triangle with the mixture. Devil's-Tongue-Jelly Sushi
is illustrated in color on page 60.

Bamboo-Leaf-wrapped Sushi (*Sasa Maki-zushi*)

24 pieces

1 2/3 cups uncooked rice, prepared as for sushi rice
12 shrimps, each about 6–7 cm long. Prepare as for Shrimp Box
   Sushi (page 89). Marinate shrimps in 4 tablespoons vinegar
   sweetened with 1 tablespoon sugar for about 5 minutes. Drain.
150 grams fresh salmon fillet. Peel off skin and remove any bones.
   Slice fillet at an angle into bite-size pieces. Salt with 2 teaspoons
   salt and allow to set for 20–30 minutes. Rinse and marinate in 4
   tablespoons vinegar sweetened with 1 tablespoon sugar for
   about 5 minutes. Drain.
24 bamboo leaves, washed and dried. When not available, any

aromatic leaves can be used, just as long as they are safe for wrapping food and not sprayed with pesticide. Aluminum foil can be used in a pinch. In Japan, persimmon and magnolia leaves are also used to wrap this type of sushi.

wasabi

vinegared water (1 cup water with 2–3 tablespoons vinegar)

Wet your hands with vinegared water. Divide rice into 24 equal portions. Shape each portion of rice into a triangular shape. Spread a little wasabi on each. (1). Top half of the rice triangles with shrimp and half with salmon. Place one triangle of rice and fish on a leaf (2). Wrap the rice and fish inside the leaf (3–4). Bamboo-Leaf-wrapped Sushi is illustrated in color on page 58.

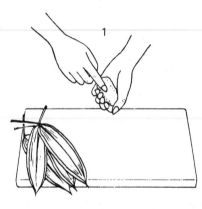
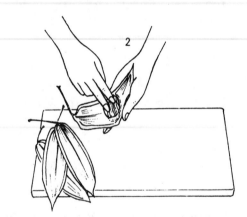
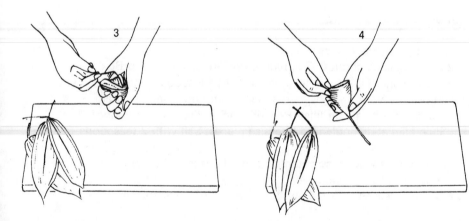

Sushi Cake

This spectacular sushi dish is quite simple to make. All you need to do is prepare your favorite scattered sushi and Narrow Rolled Sushi and combine them in an attractive way with other garnishes. This dish can be served either as a side salad or as the centerpiece of a buffet table. The size of the finished product can be varied to meet the demands of almost any party. When making a large sushi cake, an oval shape rather than the circular shape illustrated in color on page 62 is recommended.

8 rolls of Narrow Rolled Sushi (page 70), any variety
5 cups scattered sushi (page 83), any variety

Fill a mixing bowl to the brim with the scattered sushi. Turn the bowl over on the center of a large serving platter. Remove the bowl. Encircle the mound with bite-size pieces of the rolled sushi. Tie with a ribbon. Spread out the rice mound to make it the same height as the pieces of rolled sushi that surround it. Decorate as you please with other foods.

To decorate a sushi cake like that illustrated on page 62, assemble the following:

3 eggs made into thin omelets (page 8). With one omelet, prepare the chrysanthemum as for Five-color Sushi (page 85). Cut the remaining omelets into long narrow strips.
I roll of Thick Rolled Sushi (page 68), loosely stuffed and cut about 4 cm long
1–2 medium-size squids. Prepare as for Stuffed Squid Sushi (page 99). Cut the squids and spread them flat. Slash the meat at 6–7 mm intervals. Rotate the meat 90° and, holding the knife at an angle, slice into strips about 3 cm wide (1). Soak the strips in cold water for 5 minutes. Cook the strips in boiling water for about 10 seconds. (Overcooking will result in toughness.) Roll the strips to form flowers (2).

1

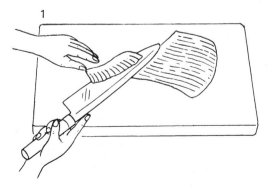

2

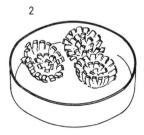

6–8 small shrimps. Prepare as for Shrimp Box Sushi (page 89), but leave them unslashed and unflattened.

fruit and leaves: maraschino cherries (or strawberries), orange segments, chrysanthemum leaves

Following the illustration, arrange the above ingredients on the cake. Place the 4-cm-long piece of Thick Rolled Sushi in the center and rest the omelet chrysanthemum on top.

Serving Suggestions

Sushi can turn any meal into a very special and memorable event. Any of the varieties of sushi included in this book—artfully arranged on trays or platters—will delight your family or guests. These dishes can be a welcome change from your regular fare, and, when entertaining, they will free you from the busyness that always comes when serving hot foods. For special occasions that celebrate a particular event, such as a birthday or anniversary, the colorful and grand sushi cake described on page 107 can serve as a fitting (and edible) centerpiece.

Don't be fooled into thinking that the lack of proper Japanese ingredients will stop you from serving sushi. Granted, some sushi ingredients are difficult to obtain. But it is also true that sushi can be made with many of the ingredients that you have around the house. In addition, a quick trip to your local market, your thinking cap on your head, will give you all sorts of good ideas. Avocado, cucumber, carrot, lettuce, broccoli, celery, parsley, and sprouts from the produce department (or your own garden), and boiled ham, cooked sausage, cold roast beef and pork, and canned salmon, crab, tuna, or sardines make excellent toppings or fillings for sushi. Devising new sushi dishes with any of these ingredients will add new dimensions to this Japanese delicacy. With ingenuity, inventiveness, and improvisation, you can devise a sushi dish of your own, a specialty that adds variety to your menu and offers a new taste experience to your guests.

In Japan, the so-called "westernized" sushi dishes—those that use Western ingredients—are becoming more and more popular. For example, sushi rice rolled up in a leaf of lettuce instead of the traditional nori has even acquired a name of its own. All you need to do is ask for *sarada maki* (salad-roll sushi) at a sushi shop and without a moment's hesitation, the chef will prepare this new variety for you. You might even try dipping your salad-roll sushi in mayonnaise or some other Western-style dip instead of soy sauce, as some sushi enthusiasts have begun to do recently.

For an informal gathering of friends, Hand-rolled Sushi served with warmed sakè and hot tea makes for a convivial atmosphere. Sitting around a table and rolling up nori, rice, and filling, as the conversation turns from subject to subject, is great fun. If it's a cold night, a bowl of hot soup, served after everyone has finished nibbling, will warm the guests and help to perk up the conversation. A luncheon gathering calls for decorative and artful arrangements of finger sushi and/or rolled sushi.

Japanese children are great sushi fans. Why not follow their example and serve sushi at a children's party? Rolled sushi made with ham, cheese, or sweetened, rolled omelets served for lunch on a summer day will be a welcome relief from the heat. Several easy-to-eat varieties of sushi made with these ingredients, arranged on colorful plates in the shapes of plants and animals, will surprise and delight children the world over.

Taking sushi on your next picnic will make for a nice change from the usual sandwich. Fish and other fillings that spoil quickly should be avoided, however. The sushi varieties to tuck in a picnic basket or boxed lunch are those made with cooked and seasoned ingredients. These varieties, coincidentally, improve in flavor with time. Candidates for such a lunch are pressed sushi such as Mackerel Stick Sushi or Sea Bream Pressed Sushi, rolled sushi made with vegetable fillings, Devil's-Tongue-Jelly Sushi, or Fox Sushi. No tableware is necessary except, perhaps, wooden chopsticks that can be thrown away. Plates, too, can be dispensed with if the sushi is packed in individual boxes. Once you've finished your sushi snack, all you need to do is throw your boxes and used chopsticks in the trash can.

For these or any other occasions on which you serve sushi, dampened cloths or paper napkins should be handy for diners to wipe their fingers on as they eat.

Beverages

When you enter a Japanese sushi shop, the *itamae*, or sushi chef, welcomes you with a hearty *Irasshai!* As you gaze about the interior, a small damp towel, steaming hot or ice-cold depending on the season, is placed on a long, sparkling clean, wooden counter to indicate where you should sit. While you wipe your hands, your eyes take in the long glass cases that cover mounds of neatly stacked fish fillets, shellfish, vegetables, and other sushi ingredients. When the itamae who will serve you looks your way in anticipation of your first order, he will ask, *O-nomimono wa?* (What will you have to drink?) and place before you a tall, hefty cup of piping hot tea.

If your answer to the itamae's question is tea, this first cup will sit by your side and will be replenished now and then as your meal progresses. Tea goes particularly well with sushi. A sip of tea taken just before eating a morsel of sushi will freshen your palate and allow you to better appreciate the delicate flavor of the rice and topping.

If you prefer an alcoholic beverage, that, too, will be brought to you. Sakè, beer, whiskey (on the rocks or in a highball), or even wine goes well with sushi. If the itamae is properly attentive, he, or one of his assistants, will see that your glass or sakè cup is never empty.

Sushi purists tend to favor tea and sakè when they go out on the town to enjoy their favorite meal. Most would agree that the flavors of these two beverages best complement the flavors of all types of sushi.

Tea   To accompany a sushi meal, select a lower-priced, full-bodied Japanese tea such as *bancha* or *hojicha*, or the slightly higher quality *sencha*. The green tea known as *gyokuro* is delicious. In fact, it is too delicious, and its sweet flavor does not go well with the taste of fish.

Several cups of bancha or hojicha can be brewed at one time. For each cup use about 1 1/2–2 tablespoons of tea and just a little bit less than a cup of boiling water. These amounts, however, can vary substantially depending on the quality of the tea. If you like, you can simply add boiling water to the once-used leaves in the pot for a second round of tea.

Sencha is graded according to when it was picked, the first picking being higher in quality and more expensive than the second and so on. Sencha goes particularly well with sushi. However, unlike bancha and hojicha it is brewed one cup at a time. When making sencha, warm the teapot with boiling water before putting in the leaves.

Cups for serving tea should be large, deep, and feature thick walls. Tea will stay warm for quite a long time in cups that fit this description.

Sakè Sakè, more properly *Nihonshu* (Japanese spirits), is one of the traditional alcoholic beverages of Japan. It is made from fermented rice, malt, and pure water, and can range in alcoholic content from 16% to 19%. Sakè comes in different tastes—sweet (*ama kuchi*) and dry (*kara kuchi*)—and grades—special, first, and second—according to its alcoholic content. Sakè is most often warmed to body temperature before drinking, but it is also imbibed at room temperature or ice-cold, poured over ice, depending on the season and the foods served.

To warm sakè, first pour it into a small-mouthed ceramic, glass, or metal container (one that holds a little less than 1 cup of liquid is just the right size). Next, slowly lower the filled container into a small saucepan of water that is just about to boil. Test the temperature of the sakè from time to time. Once it matches your body temperature, the sakè is ready to serve. Drink sakè from small, shallow cups, replenished frequently, while the next container of sakè is warming.

Sakè added to the water for cooking rice will add to the taste and fluffiness of the finished product. Whenever sakè is called for in a recipe, make sure to heat it before mixing it with the other ingredients. This will release the fragrance and reduce the alcoholic content. Once sakè that has been heated for drinking cools, it can be used to advantage in cooking.

Soups

There are two basic types of soup that accompany most Japanese meals, including one of sushi. One is a clear soup made of seasoned stock and several artfully arranged morsels of food; it is served before a meal to moisten the throat and whet the appetite for sakè and the meal to follow. The other is a thick soup, often made with *miso* (fermented bean paste); it is sipped during or at the end of a meal with a bowl of steaming hot rice. The soup that is served with sushi is most often of the latter, heartier type. A bowl of hot soup is the perfect accompaniment to scattered sushi; towards the end of a meal of finger sushi it is a welcome change in texture and temperature.

The recipes that follow will give you an idea of the kind of soups that best enhance the flavor of sushi. With imagination and flair they can be modified to suit your own taste.

Bean Curd and Seaweed Soup(*Tofu to Wakame no Suimono*)

4 servings

3 1/3 cups stock no. 1 (page 6)
150 grams bean curd (1/2 cake), drained and sliced into 2-cm
  cubes
7–10 grams *wakame,* cut into bite-size pieces. Wakame is available
  at Oriental provisions stores and many health-food stores. If it
  comes coated in dark gray ash, wash it thoroughly in cold water
  and soak in water for about 15 minutes to soften it. If salted,
  wash it thoroughly with cold water and soak in water for about
  5 minutes.
1 teaspoon salt
2 teaspoons sakè
1–2 teaspoons soy sauce

Place all the ingredients in a saucepan and bring to a boil. Take off
the heat and serve.

Chicken and Vegetable Clear Soup
(*Tori Sasami no Sumashi-jiru*)

4 servings

3 1/3 cups stock no. 1 (page 6)
80–100 grams chicken breast meat. Cut into short strips. Sprinkle
  with 1/2 teaspoon soy sauce and 1 teaspoon sakè. Roll the strips
  in cornstarch. Drop them into boiling water and cook for about
  2 minutes.
50 grams carrots, cut into narrow strips
2 fresh shiitake, cut into thin strips
1 teaspoon salt
2 teaspoons sakè
1–2 tablespoons soy sauce

In a large saucepan, combine the stock, carrot and shiitake strips,
salt, sakè, soy sauce, and chicken strips. Bring to a boil and
cook long enough to finish cooking the chicken meat. Pour the
soup into serving bowls and garnish with a small edible leaf or
sprout.

Clam Soup (*Hamaguri no Ushio-jiru*)

4 servings

15-cm-square piece of kombu, wiped with a damp cloth
4 cups water
1 teaspoon salt
1 teaspoon soy sauce
4 tablespoons sakè
5–6-cm length of green onion, thinly sliced and soaked in cold water
    for about 10 minutes. In Japan, use *negi;* in the West, use leek or
    the largest green onion or scallion you can find.
8 clams. Allow the clams to sit in water in a dark place, changing
    the water 2 or 3 times. This will allow them to rid themselves of
    foreign particles.

Pour the water into a large saucepan; add the kombu, clams, and
sakè and bring to a boil. Just before the soup boils, remove the
kombu. Reduce the heat. Remove any bubbles that float on the
surface. Add the soy sauce and turn off the heat. Add the sliced
green onions. Fresh sprouts can be added as a garnish to each
serving.

Egg Drop Soup (*Kakitama-jiru*)

4 servings

3 1/3 cups stock no. 1 (page 6)
1 teaspoon salt
1–2 teaspoons soy sauce
2 eggs, beaten well
10 grams snow peas, thinly sliced; or trefoil, cut into 2-cm lengths
8 narrow strips of lemon peel

Pour the stock into a saucepan, add the salt and soy sauce, and
bring to a boil. Add the eggs by slowly pouring them down a pair
of chopsticks. The soup base should continue to boil so that the
eggs will form long threads. Once the egg has set, add the snow
peas or trefoil and turn off the heat. Pour into the serving bowls,
adding two strips of lemon peel to each. Egg Drop Soup is illustrated
in color on page 56.

Instant Clear Soup (*Sokuseki Sumashi-jiru*)

4 servings

15 grams oboro kombu
5 grams bonito shavings
3 1/3 cups boiling water
1/2 sheet of nori, cut into short narrow strips
10 grams ginger root, thinly sliced and soaked in cold water for 5
   minutes
soy sauce

Place equal amounts of the oboro kombu, bonito shavings, ginger,
and soy sauce into each of the four serving bowls. Add boiling
water to each bowl. Season each serving to taste with soy sauce.
Garnish with the nori strips just before serving. A variation of this
recipe can be made by simply adding a small umeboshi to each
serving.

Mountain Yam Drop Soup (*Yamaimo no Otoshi-jiru*)

4 servings

3 1/3 cups stock no. 1 (page 6)
80 grams red miso paste. Miso is available at Oriental provisions or
   health-food stores.
200 grams mountain yam. Thickly peel and soak in vinegared water
   for about 20 minutes. Grate.
1/2 sheet of nori, cut into short narrow strips

Heat the stock in a saucepan. Add the miso and raise the heat. Turn
off the heat just before the soup boils. Pour the soup into serving
bowls and drop in the grated yam. Scatter the nori strips over the
top just before serving. Just before eating, stir the strips into the
soup.

Sources for Japanese Foods

The following stores stock authentic Japanese foods. If stores are not listed for your area, consult the yellow pages of your telephone directory under the Japanese foods, Oriental goods, and grocers-retail headings or enquire at the Japanese restaurant nearest you.

United States

Alabama

Ebino Oriental Foods
323 Air Base Blvd.
Montgomery 36108

Oriental Super Market no. 1
3480 Springhills Ave.
Mobile 36608

Arizona

Oriental Food Center
3920 Grand Ave.
Phoenix 85019

Oriental Food Store
408 W. Main
Jacksonville 72076

California

Aloha Market
900 South Harbor Blvd.
La Habra 90631

America Fish
1790 Sutter St.
San Francisco 90115

Asahi Market Co., Inc.
660 S. Oxnard Blvd.
Oxnard 93030

B. C. Market
711 N. Broadway
Los Angeles 90012

Ben's Market
16427 S. Western Ave.
Gardena 90247

Boys Market
General Office
Bin 73 Arroya Annex
Pasadena 91109

Castro City Market
40 S. Rengstorff Ave.
Mountain View 94040

Dobashi Market
240 Jackson St.
San Jose 95112

Ebisu Market
18940 Brookhurst St.
Fountain Valley 92708

Eiko Shoten
6082 University Ave.
San Diego 90502

Enbun Co.
248 E. 1st St.
Los Angeles 90012

Food Co. Market, Inc.
General Office
2211 Davie Ave.
Commerce 90040

Food Villa Inc., Store no. 5
Suite 510
1875 S. Bascom Ave.
Campbell 95005

Frank's Oriental Market
209 S. State College Blvd.
Anaheim 92806

Futaba Food Center
1507 Lincoln Ave.
Pasadena 91103

Garden Market
449 N. 10th St.
Santa Paula 93060

Golden West Food Marts
2377 W. Pico Blvd.
Los Angeles 90006

Higa Market
2313 W. Jefferson Blvd.
Los Angeles 90006

Highland Market—Kawase no. 1
407 S. Highland Blvd.
Hollywood 92632

Hillhurst Market
1801 N. Hillhurst St.
Los Angeles 90027

Hub Mart
2738 Hyperion Ave.
Los Angeles 90027

Hughes Market
General Office
2716 San Fernando Rd.
Los Angeles 90065

Ida Co.
339 E. 1st St.
Los Angeles 90012

Jim's Market
688 W. Baker St.
Costa Mesa 92627

King Food Market
2511 Sunset Blvd.
Los Angeles 90026

Kowloon Oriental Food
6836 Edinges Ave.
Huntington Beach 92647

Kyoto Gift & Food
2303 Highland Ave.
National City 92050

Marutaka Uptown Market
3041 W. Olympic Blvd.
Los Angeles 90006

Masatani Store
P.O. Box 38
Guadalupe 93434

McCowan Market no. 2
970 W. 1st St.
San Pedro 90731

Meiji Market
1569 W. Redondo Beach Blvd.
Gardena 90247

Mihama Fish Market
2601 Pacific Coast Hwy.
Torrance 90505

Miura Market
9066 Woodman Ave.
Arleta 90013

Miyako Oriental Foods, Inc.
404 Towne Ave.
Los Angeles 90013

Modern Food Market
318 E. 2nd St.
Los Angeles 90012

New Meiji Market
Pacific Square Center
1620 W. Redondo Beach Blvd.
Gardena 90247

Nippon Food Market
2935 Ball Rd.
Anaheim 92804

Oriental Gift Shop
Rt. 1, 115 W. Cuyama Ln.
Nipomo 93444

Oriental Grocery
418 Island Ave.
San Diego 92101

Ralph's Grocery Co.
General Office
P.O. Box 54143
Los Angeles 90054

Royal Food Market
11905 Santa Monica Blvd.
Los Angeles 90025

Sakae Oriental Grocery
4227 Convoy St.
San Diego 92111

K. Sakai Co.
1656 Post St.
San Francisco 90115

Sakura Oriental
4545 Centinela Ave.
Los Angeles 90066

Santo Market, Inc.
245 E. Taylor
San Jose 95112

Sawtelle Granada Market
1820 Sawtelle Blvd.
W. Los Angeles 90025

Senri Fish Market
111 N. Lincoln Ave.
Monterey Park 91754

Shi's Market
9896 Garden Grove Blvd.
Garden Grove 92641

Spartan Grocers
P.O. Box 3549–Terminal Annex
Los Angeles 90051

Spot Market
15224 S. Western Ave.
Gardena 90247

Suruki Oriental Food
1360 Broadway
Burlingame 94010

Takahashi Co.
221 S. Claremont
San Mateo 94401

Toyoko Food Market
15 W. Colorado Blvd.
Pasadena 91101

Yamasaki Grocery
1566 Santa Fe Ave.
Long Beach 90813

Colorado

Ann's Oriental Grocery
315 Arvada St.
Colorado Springs 80906

Granada Fish Market
1275 19th St.
Denver 80202

Kim Young Oriental
1444 Chester St.
Aurora 80010

Pacific Mercantile Co.
1925 Lawrence
Denver 80202

Connecticut

Kim's Oriental Foods & Gift
202 Park Rd.
West Hartford 06119

East/West Trading Co.
68 Howe St.
New Haven 06511

Delaware

Oriental Grocery
1705 Concord Pike
Wilmington 19803

District of Columbia

House of Hanna
7838 Easter Ave.
Washington 20012

Mikado Grocery
4709 Wisconsin Ave. N. W.
Washington 20016

Florida

Misako's Oriental Foods
129 New Warrington Rd.
North Pensacola 32406

Oriental Food Store
4559 Shirley Ave.
Jacksonville 32210

Oriental Market
1202 S. Dale Mabry Hwy.
Tampa 33609

Georgia

Asian Trading Co., Ltd.
2581 Piedmont Rd. N. E.
Atlanta 30324

Oriental Market
2306 Lumpkin Rd.
Augusta 30906

Seafood & Oriental Market
528 Main St.
Forest Park 30050

Hawaii, Oahu

A & W Markets
870 Kapahulu Ave.
Honolulu 96816

Big-Way Super Market
86–120 Farrington Hwy.
Waianae 96792

Big-Way Super Market
440 Kilani Ave.
Wahiawa 96786

Big-Way Super Market
94–340 Waipahu Depot St.
Waipahu 96797

Chun Hoon Super Market
1613 Nuuanu Ave.
Honolulu 96817

Emjay's
Aina Haina Shopping Center
Aina Haina 96821

Emjay's
1505 Dillingham Blvd.
Honolulu 96817

Emjay's
94–300 Farrington Hwy.
Waipahu 96797

Emjay's
110 Hekili St.
Kailua 96734

Everybody's Super Market
635 Pumehana St.
Honolulu 96824

Food City
1460 S. Beretania St.
Honolulu 96814

Food City
414 N. School St.
Honolulu 96817

Food City
Windward City Shopping Center
Kaneohe 96744

Foodland Super Market
Ala Moana Center
Honolulu 96814

Foodland Super Market
823 California Ave.
Wahiawa 96786

Foodland Super Market
Ewa Beach Shopping Center
Ewa Beach 96706

Foodland Super Market
160 Kailua Rd.
Kailua 96734

Foodland Super Market
Kalihi Shopping Center
Honolulu 96819

Foodland Super Market
2919 Kapiolani Blvd.
Honolulu 96826

Foodland Super Market
Koko Marina Shopping Center
Honolulu 96825

Foodland Super Market
Pearl City Shopping Center
Pearl City 96782

Foodland Super Market
Village Center North
Mililani Town 96789

Gem
1199 Dillingham Blvd.
Honolulu 96819

Gem
2055 Kam IV Rd.
Honolulu 96819

Gem
91–1207 Renton Rd.
Ewa Beach 96706

Gem
333 Ward Ave.
Honolulu 96814

Gibson's
2850 Pukoloa St.
Honolulu 96819

Hamada Store
885 Queen St.
Honolulu 96813

Holiday Mart
345 Hahani St.
Kailua 96734

Holiday Mart
801 Kaheka St.
Honolulu 96814

Holiday Mart
850 Kamehameha Hwy.
Pearl City 96782

Kalihi Queen's Super Market
1010 Kaili St.
Honolulu 96819

Kit's Super Market
66–190 Kamehameha Hwy.
Haieiwa 96712

Longs Drug Store
Ala Moana Center
Honolulu 96814

Longs Drug Store
143 S. Hotel St.
Honolulu 96817

Longs Drug Store
Kahala Mall Shopping Center
Honolulu 96816

Longs Drug Store
591 Kailua Rd.
Kailua 96734

Longs Drug Store
Kamehameha Shopping Center
Honolulu 96819

Longs Drug Store
Kaneohe Bay Shopping Center
Kaneohe 96744

Longs Drug Store
1330 Pali Hwy.
Honolulu 96813

Longs Drug Store
Pearl City Shopping Center
Pearl City 96782

Longs Drug Store
Pearlridge Center
Aiea 96701

Miyashiro Grocery Store
47–571 Kamehameha Hwy.
Kaneohe 96744

Moilili Store
2643 S. King St.
Honolulu 96826

P & P Super Foods
2229 N. School St.
Honolulu 96819

P & P Super Foods
3086 Waialae Ave.
Honolulu 96816

Shirokiya
Ala Moana Center
Honolulu 96814

Speedy's Super Market
99–079 Kauhale St.
Aiea 96701

Star Super Market
Kamehameha Shopping Center
Honolulu 98619

Star Super Market
46–023 Kamehameha Hwy.
Kaneohe 96744

Star Super Market
30 Kihapai St.
Kailua 96734

Star Super Market
2470 S. King St.
Honolulu 96819

Star Super Market
Pearlridge Center
Aiea 96701

Star Super Market
4211 Waialae Ave.
Honolulu 96816

Tanabe Superette
934 Keeaumoku St.
Honolulu 96814

Taniguchi Store
2065 S. Beretania St.
Honolulu 96826

Times Super Market
Aiea Shopping Center
Aiea 96701

Times Super Market
1290 S. Beretania St.
Honolulu 96814

Times Super Market
1210 Dillingham Blvd.
Honolulu 96817

Times Super Market
94–766 Farrington Hwy.
Waipahu 96797

Times Super Market
47–388 Hui Iwa
Kaneohe 96744

Times Super Market
98–1264 Kaahumanu St.
Pearl City 96782

Times Super Market
590 Kailua Rd.
Kailua 96734

Times Super Market
5140 Kalanianaole Hwy.
Honolulu 96821

Times Super Market
45–934 Kamehameha Hwy.
Kaneohe 96744

Times Super Market
1776 S. King St.
Honolulu 96817

Times Super Market
1425 Liliha St.
Honolulu 96817

Times Super Market
1173 21st Ave.
Honolulu 96816

Waimalu Super Market
Waimalu Shopping Center
Aiea 96701

The Warehouse
Moanalua Shopping Center
Aiea 96701

Idaho

Yuko's Gift
688 N. Holmes Ave.
Idaho Falls 83401

Illinois

Far East Food Co.
105 S. 5th St.
Champaign 61820

Ginza & Co.
315 E. University
Champaign 61820

Hisaya's Oriental Food
112 Homestead
Ofallon 62269

Star Market
3349 N. Clark St.
Chicago 60657

Indiana

Asia Oriental Market
2400 Yeager Rd.
West Lafayette 47906

Iowa

Tokyo Foods
1005 Pierce St.
Sioux City 51105

Kentucky

Machiko's Asian Imports & Foods
1488 Leestown Rd.
Lexington 40505

Louisiana

Korea House
615 Orange St.
New Orleans 70130

Maryland

Far East House
33 W. North Ave.
Baltimore 21201

Fumi Oriental Mart
2102 Veirs Mill Rd.
Rockville 20852

Massachusetts

House of Kim
852 Massachusetts Ave.
Lexington 02173

Mirim Trading Co., Inc.
152 Harvard Ave.
Allston 02134

Yoshinoya
36 Prospect St.
Cambridge 02139

Michigan

Mt. Fuji Oriental Foods
22040 W. 10 Mile Rd.
Southfield 48075

Oriental Food Store
18919 W. 7 Mile Rd.
Detroit 48219

Minnesota

First Oriental Food
1517 Como Ave. S. E.
Minneapolis 55454

Kim's Oriental Grocery
689 N. Snelling Ave.
St. Paul 55104

Missouri

King's Trading Inc.
3736 Broadway St.
Kansas City 64111

Maruyama Inc.
100 N. 18 St.
St. Louis 63103

Nebraska

Oriental Market
611 N. 27th St.
Lincoln 68503

Oriental Trading Co.
10525 J St.
Omaha 68127

Nevada

Oriental Food of Las Vegas
853 E. Sahara, Space E–31
Las Vegas 89109

New Jersey

Aki Oriental Food Co.
1635 Lemoine Ave.
Fort Lee 07024

Daido International
1385 16 St.
Fort Lee 07024

Miyako Oriental Foods
490 Main St.
Fort Lee 07024

Oriental Bazaar
700 Jersey Ave.
Elizabeth 07201

New Mexico

Yonemoto Brothers
8725 4th St. N. W.
Albuquerque 87114

New York

AC Gift
565 Boston Post Rd.
Portchester 10573

AC Gift
2642 Central Park Ave.
Yonkers 10710

Ajiya Mart Inc.
41–75 Bowne St.
Flushing 11354

Daido
41–54 Main St.
Flushing 11355

Harumi
318 W. 231 St.
Bronx 10463

Katagiri and Co., Inc.
224 E. 59th St.
New York 10022

Lee's Oriental Gift & Food Shop
3053 Main St.
Buffalo 14208

Meidiya
18 N. Central Ave.
Hartsdale, 10530

New World Oriental Food Center Co.
103–37 Queens Blvd.
Forest Hills 11375

Nippon-Do Food, Inc.
82–69 Parsons Blvd.
Jamaica 11432

K. Tanaka Co., Inc.
326 Amsterdam Ave.
New York 10023

Tomon
5678 Mosholu Ave.
Bronx 10471

Tsujimoto Oriental Art Gifts & Food,
  Inc.
6530 Seneca
Elma 14059

North Carolina

Asia Market
1325 Buck Jones Rd.
Raleigh 27606

Oriental Food Mart
803 N. Main St.
Spring Lake 28390

Ohio

Dayton Oriental Foods
812 Xenia Ave.
Dayton 45410

Soya Food Products Inc.
2356 Wyoming Ave.
Cincinnati 45214

Oklahoma

Japan Imported Foods
808 N. W. 6th St.
Oklahoma City 73106

Oregon

Anzen Imports
736 N. E. Union Ave.
Portland 97232

Fred Meyers
11425 S. W. Beaverton-Hillsdale Hwy.
Beaverton 97005

Fred Meyers
777 Kings Blvd.
Corvallis 97330

Shin Shin Market
2001 S. E. Stark St.
Portland 97214

Pennsylvania

Asia Products Corp.
226 N. 10th St.
Philadelphia 19107

Imported Food Bazaar
2000 Market St.
Camp Hill 17011

Sambok Market
1737 Penn Ave.
Pittsburgh 15222

Rhode Island

Persimmon Oriental Market
University Heights Shopping Center
Providence 02906

South Carolina

Chieko Hardy
226 Jamaica St.
Columbia 29206

Oriental Food & Gift
4252 Rivers Ave.
N. Charleston 29405

Tennessee

Orient Food Store
1513 Church St.
Nashville 37203

Pan-Asia Food Market
1905 W. End Ave.
Nashville 37203

Park & Shop Oriental
3664 Summer Ave.
Memphis 38122

Texas

Asiatic Imports
821 Chartres
Houston 77003

Edo-Ya Oriental Market
223 Farmers Branch Shopping Center
Dallas, Texas 75234

Mihama-Ya Oriental Foods
360 Inwood Village
Dallas 75209

Nippon Daido U.S.A., Inc.
11138 W. Heimer St.
Houston 77042

Utah

Sage Farm Market
1515 S. Main
Salt Lake City 84115

Virginia

Asia Center Discount Oriental
    Groceries
303 W. Broad St.
Falls Church 22046

Super Asian Market
2719 Wilson Blvd.
Arlington 22201

Tokyo Market
5312 Virginia Beach Blvd.
Virginia Beach 23462

Washington

Beacon Market
2500 Beacon Street
Seattle 98144

Kiyo's Sea Food
3203 Beacon Street
Seattle 98144

Miya Mura Food Mart
5261 University Way N. E.
Seattle 98105

Public Warehouse Mart
W. 3330 Central Ave.
Spokane 99208

Uwajimaya, Inc.
6th St. & S. King St.
Seattle 98104

Wisconsin

K. P. Oriental Grocery & Gift
821 N. 27 St.
Milwaukee 53208

Peace Oriental Foods & Gift
4250 W. Fond du Lac Ave.
Milwaukee 53216

Canada

Alberta

Allwest Supermarket
5720 Silverspring Blvd. N. W.
Calgary

Edmonton Co-op no. 3
17010 90th Ave.
Edmonton

Woodwards
Chinook Shopping Centre
Calgary

Woodwards
3850 98th St.
Edmonton

British Columbia

Canada Safeway no. 118
1300 Lonsdale
North Vancouver

Fairway Market
272 Gorge Rd.
Victoria

Mihamaya
392 Powell St.
Vancouver

Shimizu Shoten
349 E. Hastings St.
Vancouver

Woodwards
Coquitlam Centre
Port Coquitlam

New Brunswick

House of Juliet, Ltd.
606 Albert St.
Fredericton

Nova Scotia

Rose Marie Oriental Gourmet
1532 Queen St.
Halifax

Ontario

Furuya Trading Co., Ltd.
460 Dundas St. W.
Toronto

Iwaki Japanese Food Store
2627 Yonge St.
Toronto

Nakanishi Japan Food Store
465 Somerset St. W.
Ottawa

Yanagawa Japanese Foods
639 Upper James St.
Hamilton

Québec

Miyamoto Provisions
382 Victoria Ave.
Montreal

Recipe Index

The "weathermark" identifies this book as a production of Weatherhill, Inc., publishers of fine books on Asia and the Pacific. Typography and book design by Meredith Weatherby.